Rangda,
Bali's Queen of the Witches

Rangda,
Bali's Queen of the Witches

Claire Fossey

White Lotus Press

© 2008 by Claire Fossey. All rights reserved.

White Lotus Co., Ltd
G.P.O. Box 1141
Bangkok 10501
Thailand

Tel.   (66) 0-38239-883-4
Fax   (66) 0-38239-885
E-mail   ande@loxinfo.co.th
Website http://thailine.com/lotus

Printed in Thailand

Designed and typeset by COMSET Limited Partnership

ISBN   978-974-480-139-5   pbk.   White Lotus Co., Ltd., Bangkok

Contents

List of Illustrations vii
Foreword ix
Acknowledgements xiii
Introduction xv

1. Situating Rangda in Past Discourses 1

2. Rangda's Singular Appearance and Multiple Identities 7

3. Truly Evil or Not?: Philosophical and Ethical Dimensions of Rangda 37

4. Implications of Rangda for Constructing the Feminine 47

5. Conclusion 67

Notes 77
Glossary of Balinese Terms 81
Works Cited 83
Index 89

List of Illustrations

List of Figures (Photographs 2, 4–5, 7–10 by Claire Fossey)
1. *Balinese "Witches"* by Ida Bagus Nyoman Tjeta (1937). Originally published in Hildred Geertz, *Images of Power: Balinese Paintings Made for Gregory Bateson and Margaret Mead* (Honolulu: University of Hawaii Press, 1994). Courtesy of Hildred Geertz and the Bateson-Mead collection 8
2. Rangda wrapped in *poleng* 12
3. *"Tjerita Derman" A woman, possibly Sri Tanjung, travels to purgatory. On her path are Sang Suratma, scribe of sins, and Sang Jogormanik, who dictates punishments* by an unknown painter (before 1942). Courtesy of Leo Haks 21
4. Rangda, Ubud Pura Dalem 29
5. Rangda, Peliatan cemetery 30
6. *Cremation preparations observed by sorcerers* by Ida Bagus Putu Blatjok (1936). Originally published in Hildred Geertz, *Images of Power: Balinese Paintings Made for Gregory Bateson and Margaret Mead* (Honolulu: University of Hawaii Press, 1994). Courtesy of Hildred Geertz and the Bateson-Mead collection 42
7. Barong procession at Pura Luhur 44
8. Rangda procession at Pua Luhur 44
9. Rangda masks for sale, Ubud 68
10. Temporary storage in Ubud Pura Dalem 74

List of Plates
1. *Barong I* by Hendra Gunawan (1974). Originally published in Agus Dermawan T. and Dr. Astri Wright *Hendra Gunawan: A Great Modern Indonesian Painter*

List of Illustrations

(Singapore, Ir. Ciputra Foundation, 2001). Courtesy of the Ciputra Education Foundation
2. *Scene from a dramatic performance in which men who try to kill the witch-goddess Rangda turn their krisses on themselves under her spell* by Ida Bagus Made Togog (before 1942). Courtesy of Leo Haks
3. *Rangda, goddess of sorcery, bestows her blessing on a man meditating in her temple* by Ida Bagus Made Togog (before 1942). Courtesy of Leo Haks
4. *Dancer Stepping on My Head* by Kartika Affandi (1995). Courtesy of the artist

Foreword

Bali is known to millions of people around the world who have visited or heard about the small island. Drawn by its actively performative and intensely artistic ways of making meaning of the world, scholars, artists, journalists and visitors alike have long been fascinated by Balinese culture. Never static or monolithic, Bali demonstrates a continuously evolving practice of weaving and reweaving traditions and innovations into new, hybrid patterns which in varying degrees combine freshness with time-sanctioned integrity. Bali also supports creative practices in many fields which address challenges that are no longer local and contained but concern us all, globally. In recent years, the island has become known to the world in new ways, with the unprecedented global media coverage in the aftermath of the terrorist bombing in October 2002 and around the global environmental conference in December 2007.

Since the early twentieth century and the beginnings of sustained international tourism to the island—today one of Indonesia's thirty-three provinces—tourist literature about this Hindu-Balinese island in the midst of a largely Muslim nation has swamped the guidebook shelves of shops and libraries. More recently, Bali figures prominently on the Internet: Googling it currently gets 52 million hits. Along with Java and other islands and ethnic cultures of Indonesia, Bali has also been the subject of on-going scholarly studies by outsiders working more or less closely with insiders for well over a century.

But touristic information is nearly always too shallow and simplistic and scholarly sources are nearly always too difficult for the general public to find and absorb. To contribute to enhancing the world-mindedness of people everywhere, not only those enrolled in academic course-work, it is the in-between literature that is needed: writing that is historically, culturally and analytically informed but composed in accessible language and published in a format that travels with

Foreword

ease—writing that does not limit itself to narrowly framed scholarly dimensions and does not disdain the popular and contemporary.

Claire Fossey's new book fulfils these desires. She offers, here, the first sustained study in many decades of Rangda, the most dramatically and horrifically masked, dressed and choreographed, acted, painted and sculpted, among Bali's many mythological characters. Fossey picks up on earlier discussions of Rangda in writings by scholars of dance-drama, religion, anthropology, and art history. She skillfully develops her interdisciplinary text (which includes oral history—adding the voices and views of a selection of Balinese men and women she interviewed), combining all of her varied data into a cohesive and sensitive analysis. In the process, and without the sensationalist simplifications so often encountered where statements are made across gaps of culture, space, and race, the reader will emerge with a better sense of Bali, specifically, as well as a clearer grasp of the general principle of multiplicity, illustrated by the multiple meanings individual images hold both over time as well as horizontally, among members of the same cultural and historical moment.

Rangda, one could argue, holds an even more dominant position in Bali than Kali or Durga in India do, in the totality of Hindu philosophy, theatre, and art. The very fact that she, despite her undeniable importance, has not been the subject of a recent monograph bearing her name, illustrates that valuable research remains to be done in certain fields, also at the MA level, in the hands of the right person. It also underscores the importance of this publication. Claire Fossey's *Rangda, Bali's Queen of the Witches*, demonstrates that an advanced student with an eye for holes and potentials in the body of academic expertise, and with the requisite analytical skills and dedication, can identify a topic for research that may merit publication and contribute to the state of knowledge. It is gratifying to see a book like this be published in a field like Southeast Asian art history, by necessity a highly inter-disciplinary field, and one of the youngest additions to the streams of Asian art history, all too long over-shadowed by the grand narratives of China and India. Bali provides one of hundreds of case-studies for how Southeast Asian indigenous cultures adopted, adapted and incorporated influences from abroad over thousands of years without fear of loss of identity or a too-rigid definition of the same, and often with remarkable tolerance and skill—a process the rapidly pluralizing parts of the world might learn much from. Within these larger Southeast Asian case-studies, Fossey's study of Rangda provides a specific framing of a similar practice.

It is particularly exciting to me, long dedicated to the idea that subtle and sophisticated ideas do not require inaccessibly obtuse language for expression, to commend Claire Fossey and White Lotus Press for bringing out publications that can serve both the academic and the non-specialist, the intelligent general reader

Foreword

with an interest in Southeast Asia. I can just imagine members of both groups (who of course in reality inhabit the same continuum) reading this book side by side on airplanes, on tropical beaches, in internet cafés, and while waiting for the dance performance in Peliatan or Ubud or to begin.

A final image comes to mind. It is of Rangda, suddenly stopped in the midst of a charge at the Barong—one foot raised, long protruding tongue swinging pendulum like, then slowly coming to a rest. Gingerly, Rangda picks up a copy of this book, her long, white, flat nails flapping. Turning it over, she cocks her eye-bulging head at the energy and attention flowing to her, around her, from its printed pages — energy like an offering which redeems her from the stamp of pure evil. This unexpected pause in Rangda's performance provides a brief interlude before the magnificent witch / mother / regeneratrix resumes her macabre but necessary dance of destroying and awakening, of puzzlement and clarification.

My thoughts return to the scholars and travelers who set off on journeys that take them far from their familiar and the necessary critiques ensuing generations provide. I've learned in Java and Bali the idea of treating the "ancestors" with respect; to remember, in this case, that it takes courage to become a bridge (as all the writers cited in this book did and Claire Fossey with them) and realize that the act of bridging does not need to entail claims to full knowledge and insight. A bridge only needs to know, and be able to hold firmly onto, the edge on either side. Its span represents a leap across and into the unknown. But in making this leap, it provides passage for others whose explorations will be easier, travel further and delve deeper because of the service of that bridge.

Astri Wright
Professor of Southeast Asian Art
University of Victoria, BC, Canada
January 2008

Acknowledgements

This book would not have been possible without the help of the many individuals who were willing to share their knowledge and their time. I would like to give special thanks to Dr. Astri Wright for the passion and support she offered from the early stages of thesis preparation through to the translation of that thesis into book form. My sincere thanks also to Dr. Hildred Geertz for her encouragement during the editing process.

The original research in Bali would not have been possible without the help of my assitant and interpreter I Wayan Sugita. I am most grateful also to the people in Bali who shared with me their thoughts and their stories. Without them, this book would not exist.

Finally, I wish to thank my parents and my friends for their continued interest, understanding and support. It is my hope that this book will give back some small part of all that has been given to me throughout the process of its creation.

Introduction

The figure of Rangda, Queen of the Witches, looms large in the image culture of Bali. Her distinctive features make her instantly recognizable even to those with only a passing awareness of who she is and yet, despite this visual consistency, the many associations that might be brought about by an encounter with Rangda suggest there is much more to her than a frightening mask. Hers is a figure that can be painted in many colors. She may hold the place of a storybook witch or a character in a dance drama at the same time that she functions as a deity, a powerful symbol of the forces of chaos, or an image of the exotic with which to sell Balinese culture to tourists. These are shifting, overlapping roles whose currency varies from one point in time to another and from individual context and person within each point in time.

Rangda was one of the first subjects seriously to interest foreign artists and writers in Bali during the first half of the twentieth century. The image of Rangda was at that time, and remains still, one of the most pervasive in island's symbol-rich culture. As John Stephen Lansing has noted, "Rangda and Barong are compelling, almost irresistible symbols and nearly everyone who studies Balinese culture eventually writes about them."[1] The study of Bali by non-Balinese—in a range of modes including amateur, colonial, scholarly, and touristic—has grown a good deal since German artist Walter Spies came to live in the village of Ubud in the late 1920s. And yet despite the many changes in the approaches taken by anthropologists and other writers contributing to the discourse on the society and culture of Bali, surprisingly little has been done to update early ideas about Rangda and to question whether they still hold true.

While I do not suggest that these early views were necessarily wrong, I will argue that they are in some respects outdated. Although Spies worked via his painting and photography to challenge the sometimes vulgar image of Bali propagated by the media of the time, the image of a vibrant folk culture with which he sought to

Introduction

replace it was itself strongly influenced by his own personal vision. Spies was given a free hand in his work on the pseudo-documentary film *Island of the Demons*, a story in which the happiness of two lovers is threatened by a Rangda-like witch, because the filmmakers Victor Baron von Plessen and Dr Dahlseim themselves knew little of Bali and relied heavily on Spies's impressions from his time there. Adrian Vickers noted that Spies was himself influenced in style and possibly even subject matter by the work of his friend Friedrich Murnau, director of the 1922 horror classic *Nosferatu*.[2] Envisioned by Spies, Rangda was an exotic and mysterious being of an almost Gothic sort.

For the American anthropologist Margaret Mead, and subsequently for her colleague Jane Belo whom Mead encouraged to undertake a study of Rangda, this figure of the Queen of the Witches was in many regards seen as a perfect case study within psychoanalytic theory of the fear aspect of the mother figure. This theoretical framework becomes problematic for the present day, given the serious critique of Freudian theories in the latter half of the twentieth century, beginning as early as Carl Jung and culminating in post-colonial criticism.

Later anthropologists such as Lansing and Vickers have in the past expressed concerns regarding the way in which one or two popular interpretations of Rangda have been privileged over others.[3] However, since Rangda was not the central focus of their studies, they did not pursue the concern they raised beyond a few explanatory sentences. My purpose here is to pick up some of those threads and to explore further some of the alternate ways in which Rangda may be viewed.

This book presents an interdisciplinary art historical discussion of Rangda; that is to say, I write as an art historian but draw upon sources in anthropology as well as religious, gender, and cultural studies. A pluralistic approach is appropriate, even necessary for a figure such as Rangda with her many overlapping identities. I link Rangda's appearance not to a single identity, as art history has arguably done in the past, but to the many identities suggested by anthropological writing, by an examination of a number of artworks in which she occurs, and by my own contacts in Bali. This link serves as a jumping-off point for an exploration of the Queen of the Witches and her various possible implications for contemporary Balinese culture, but one that neither seeks to romanticize her nor views her through a Freudian filter.

Having set these parameters, I must acknowledge that even the use of the word "witch" with regards to Rangda is suspect. Although Rangda is often referred to as a witch, as this often appears to be the simplest substitute in English for the Balinese *leyak*, an individual who has studied black magic and uses it destructively;

Introduction

the connotations of the word "witch" in Balinese culture are not, of course, the same as those in European cultures. Unlike witchcraft in the context of Christian culture where the practice of sorcery is considered anathema to the worship of God, in Bali "acts of sorcery are hardly distinguishable from acts of worship, except in intent and consequences."[4]

The word "witch" nonetheless appears throughout this book as this was the word most often used by interviewees as an appropriate translation for *leyak*. It is also the word that appears most frequently with regards to Rangda in both tourist and academic literature on Bali. This choice may appear to run counter to the aim to avoid exoticizing the figure of Rangda, especially when it appears in a title such as *Rangda, Bali's Queen of the Witches*. However, the fact that "witch" was used by my contacts interchangeably with *leyak* and that they would also on occasion use such terms as Queen of the Witches suggests that they were not uncomfortable with this term. That non-Balinese may thus tend initially to impose the model of the witch with warts, pointed hat, and broomstick from the Euro-North American cultural tradition onto the Balinese entity is problematic, but not as much as it may have been in the past. This is in large part due to the efforts of those feminists and modern witches who have been working to reclaim the word, allowing it a much more inclusive definition. Thus, rather than interpret Rangda according to the model of the Wicked Witch of the West, I would ask the reader to broaden the idea of witch to include the Balinese model.

Even when Rangda is clearly presented in an Indonesian context, it can be difficult to gain an understanding of who she is or just what she represents. Her mask is a sacred object intended to hold her spirit during ceremonies, but at the same time imitations of this mask are readily available to be viewed in exhibition dance performances and purchased in souvenir shops. Her image has been rendered by Balinese artists both to be used locally and to be presented to foreign scholars such as Mead, by eminent Javanese painters such as Hendra Gunawan or Kartika Affandi for exhibition and collection, and even by the creators of pamphlets intended to portray—and to market—Balinese culture to tourists from abroad. One does not need to look far beyond Bali itself to find points of disjunction between the various portrayals.

For the sake of creating a streamlined and sensational image, the tourist industry actively propagates the notion that Rangda is evil. Tourist pamphlets and books found in Bali describe her as a practitioner of black magic who dwells in darkness, or in even broader strokes as "the evil, hair-raising witch, a symbol of villainy, hatred, lust, jealousy and everything else that's nasty."[5] Scholarly works by non-Balinese

Introduction

occasionally hint at a more multi-dimensional character for Rangda, but they also tend to use the above manner of a description as a default when space dictates. The literature on Bali either speaks of Rangda predominantly as "the most evil of all,"[6] or is simply silent regarding the extent to which she is actually perceived as a negative, bad, or undesirable being. And yet when I asked Rucina Ballinger, co-author of *Balinese Dance, Drama and Music: A Guide to the Performing Arts of Bali* and a woman who has long lived in Bali, whether Rangda was always evil, she corrected me, saying that "many Balinese would argue that Rangda is *not* evil. She is part of the balance." To the Balinese people I subsequently interviewed during my time there in 1999, Rangda came across as a complex figure playing a necessary part in the balance between light and dark and in the cycle of life and death.

The one-dimensional depiction of Rangda appearing in the pamphlet cited above is indicative of the material written for a general audience made up of tourists. It is composed with the assumption that visitors may only have the time or the attention span for a few words. Brevity is of the essence in the context of reading material designed with tourists in mind, and Rangda described briefly appears as above. Naturally, anthropologists writing about Bali have not taken this approach; however, when they speak of Rangda at all, they have tended to deal with her solely as she appears in the realm of dance.

Art history has in the past ignored Rangda outside the realm of basic iconography. When she appeared at all, it would be either too briefly to explore her in any detail, or in a context in which the history of art as an exploration of visual culture was not the main focus. Rangda's appearance in sacred dance has often been touched upon, but only to the extent that it illustrates points made with regards to iconography. For example, her large teeth may be pointed to as a symbol of the bestial, or the flame atop her head as a representation of her magical powers. Art history left all other avenues of discussion—Rangda's role outside the boundaries of the dance stage, the possible reasons behind her construction, the place she holds in the imaginations of individual Balinese people and how this is manifested, and so forth—to the fields of anthropology and religious studies, which have in turn only given her passing attention.

My work straddles several fields, but I feel this is necessary in order to deal with a figure such as Rangda, most often encountered through the media of visual or performance art, but that also has a complex and wide-reaching history and present-day influence beyond these realms in her mythology, ritual, and the ways in which her archetype resonates for the Balinese people. It is not sufficient to speak of Rangda simply in terms of iconography if one wishes to gain an understanding of her shifting identities and their numerous possible perceptions. Together with her traditional foe, the Barong, Rangda is, according to Lansing "possibly" one of "the most popular symbols among the Balinese."[7] The degree to which people in Bali today still believe in Rangda's power more than three decades after the publication of Lansing's book may vary, but her image and attributes remain widely known throughout the culture.

The initial research for the Master's thesis on which this book is based was inspired by a number of key questions. For example, what negotiations between good and evil may exist behind Rangda's deceptively straightforward iconography? If the face of evil is an old woman, does it follow that Balinese culture condemns female power as a negative force, or that it has an ageist bias against women? To what extent do the individuals I interviewed perceive Rangda as a force of evil in contemporary society? What currency does she have today? How do individuals in Bali feel about the adoption of Rangda by the tourist industry as one of the key symbols by which Bali is marketed? How might a person's perception of this alter according to the spatial context of the interview?

During a summer in Bali in 1999, I conducted interviews with a selection of men and women, almost all Balinese, from various spheres of life. I would like to be able to say that I held few preconceived notions when approaching this project, but my views from the outset were necessarily colored by my cultural background and by an on-going interest in the stories of witches from a variety of other cultures. I would like to add that my findings were based purely and objectively on the data I collected, but a reader would immediately recognize this as an impossible claim. First of all, as a Canadian of European descent, I am not writing from the vantage point of a Balinese or even an Indonesian. My own cultural heritage cannot help but inform my interpretation of the culture of Bali. As Clifford Geertz has written in his essay "'Native's Point of View': Anthropological Understanding": "The ethnographer does not, and, in my opinion, largely cannot, perceive what his informants perceive. What he perceives, and that uncertainly enough, is what they perceive "with"—or "by means of," or "through" . . . or whatever the word should be. In the country of the blind . . . the one-eyed is not king, he is spectator."[8]

In other words, and to state the obvious, a researcher coming from outside the culture of Bali cannot expect to perceive Balinese realities as people born or residing in Bali would. I use the plural of reality because if Balinese culture is to be understood as non-monolithic, then it follows that all individuals will not perceive "Balineseness" in the same way; the reality of a Brahmin priest is going to differ from that of a low-caste widow. Differences in age, gender, caste, or geographic placement all have the potential to alter perceptions vastly. Some generalizations are necessary when one is studying a topic, as there would never be enough time to interview everyone (assuming everyone would even want to provide testimony) or enough space to record every view. At the same time, there is a considerable potential for misrepresentation in a monolithic version of Balinese culture(s).

For example, while it may be acceptable to say that Rangda is a pervasive force throughout much of Bali, it would be misleading to say that the Balinese all believe in Rangda as this does not take into account some regions, most obviously the Muslim part of North Bali that does not include her as a major figure in its mythology. Cautiousness with regards to generalizations and openness to multiplicities are especially important for an outsider who cannot expect to be able to perceive all of the often-subtle differences between that which is widespread and that which exists on the individual level.

The very fact that this study has been undertaken by a Canadian rather than a Balinese could conceivably be said to contribute to the propagation of the academic discourse on Bali that has been conducted outside Bali by non-Balinese whose voices are too often privileged over the voices of the Balinese themselves. This is an undesirable position for anyone who sees equal access to self-representation as an ideal, but I am unconvinced that the solution is to be found in silence. Perhaps the best one can do at present is to make the writer's cultural vantage point as obvious to the reader as possible. Throughout this book, therefore, I make references to aspects of Euro-North American popular culture which have been triggered by association during my research. These are not included with any intention of flippancy, but rather function as an acknowledgement of the practical fact that the majority of the audience for this book is likely to be made up of people with backgrounds not wholly dissimilar to my own—or at least more closely linked to mine than the people who generated the figural meanings of Rangda—and as a constant reminder to that audience of my own inherent cultural bias.

Cross-cultural analogies can also be a useful aid to the understanding of foreign concepts. Jane Belo made just such an analogy when she likened Rangda to Santa Claus, the Tax Collector, and the Angel of Death rolled into one.[9] My North American popular culture references could also be said to take a cue from James A. Boon's approach in *Affinities and Extremes: Crisscrossing the Bittersweet Ethnology of East Indies History, Hindu-Balinese Culture, and Indo-European Allure*, specifically the chapter entitled "Siwaic Semiotics: Allegorical Machineries, Spatial Desituations, Polycosmology, Parodic Performance," in that it emulates conventions found in Balinese performance traditions. The use of laughter and the familiar often has the ability to provide an antidote to wariness of and even suspicion toward the unfamiliar. In dance, it is the role of the clown or servant characters to break into the action at intervals in order to reiterate in the vernacular, and make fun of, the complex ideas presented by the main characters. Similar tactics may be used in writing. In addition to disseminating sometimes difficult concepts accessibly, this approach also serves to demystify the subject through promoting empathy. This is especially important in a study that attempts to avoid exoticizing Rangda, and hence the Balinese, as an example of the sort of "Oriental horrific" as writers in the time of Walter Spies or Miguel Covarrubias did.

With regards to my own research in Bali, I need to be clear as to the scope of my work in the field. My goal was never to create a definitive study of Rangda, but to provide an additional page to the past scholarship in which she appears. My interest has been in personal perceptions of Rangda, especially those of individuals with whom I had the opportunity to interact socially on more than one occasion. For this reason, combined with only a basic knowledge of Indonesian, which necessitated cooperation with a local translator, I did not interview a large sampling of individuals throughout the island. Most of the work was done in Ubud, with visits to some of the surrounding villages as well as excursions to places such as Tabanan or Klungkung.

Another factor taken into account is the matter of individual experience and opinion. This comes into play in any study involving perceptions held by people, Balinese or otherwise, toward a given subject. It would be too easy to dehumanize the individuals interviewed by compiling the data collected and placing it all under the heading of one culture group, in other words, rendering Balinese culture monolithic. This has been precisely the approach taken by the tourist industry, fueled by the desire to simplify Bali's cultural identity into something that can be easily packaged and sold. The commodification of cultures can be found to a greater or lesser extent worldwide, but the intensive tourism in Bali has caused the effects to be particularly noticeable there. I naturally do not presume the findings from my work in the field to encompass the views of all or even most Balinese on the subject of Rangda. Rather, they reflect the views of a limited cross section, a small number of individuals as they chose to transmit them to me at a particular point in time.

The approach of tourist presentation and consumption runs counter to that taken by academic writing about Bali in the last decade or so, where pains have been taken to underline the complexity of Balinese culture. This has not always been the case, especially among writers who were not academics. Covarrubias' *Island of Bali* is a case in point. Covarrubias was not an academic but, like Spies, an artist. In spite of this, the popularity of his book over the years lent his words a weight that rivaled that of more clearly scholarly studies. Boon has pointed out the tendency of Covarrubias to make generalizations for the sake of presenting a more seamless narrative in *Affinities and Extremes*. According to Covarrubias, for example:

> "The Balinese say that a house, like a human being, has a head—the family shrine; arms—the sleeping-quarters and social parlor; a navel—the courtyard; sexual organs— the gate; legs and feet—the kitchen and the granary; the anus—the pit in the backyard where the refuse is disposed of" (1937: 88). Balinese, at least select ones do indeed say (and write) such things, as do other Indonesians who like to liken domiciles to crocodiles, ships, macrocosms, intercourse, and so on. Yet these tropes are just that—tropes—and are not to be generalized as a culture's tacit creed or central doctrine.[10]

In the essentializing mode, an anecdote told to me by the painter I G.A.K. Murniasih (1966–2006, known to many as Murni) about being terrified by an apparition of Rangda she saw when returning from the cinema one night with her boyfriend turns into a statement along the lines of: Balinese people are frightened of Rangda, the widow-witch who may periodically appear as a nightmare vision on a dark, deserted road or elsewhere, and is capable of causing terrible illness. Such a statement does two things. First, it erases the subject's identity: in this case, a woman from West Bali who spent her childhood in Sulawesi, is a divorcee, and practices non-traditional painting. It erases her identity as an individual capable of autonomous actions and opinions that need not invariably be a function of her identity as a Balinese. Secondly, the statement would suggest that all Balinese people relate to Rangda in the same way.

Unni Wikan opens *Managing Turbulent Hearts: A Balinese Formula for Living* with a quotation from Mark Hobart: "I do not wish to suggest that there is any essential Balinese culture. There are only the myriad statements and actions in which people living on the island of Bali, and calling themselves Balinese, engage."[11] For Rangda, there are many perspectives possible and many interpretations based on them. However, as Rangda is unique to Bali, it is still in a sense possible to describe all these differences as fitting into a single, unified whole under the heading Balinese culture. Such an approach could effectively gloss over the multitude of different life experiences that cause people in Bali to perceive Rangda in the various ways discussed in this book. At the same time, a researcher, both in the library and in the field, is constantly confronted with just such generalizations. For example, Lansing writes in an essay entitled "Barong and Rangda: Balinese

Introduction

Symbolism of Evil" that: "The Barong, *to the Balinese* [emphasis added], is the arch foe of Rangda, the witch who controls black magic and delights in feeding on the entrails of young children."[12] Statements of this kind—and Lansing is not alone in making them—imply that every person in Bali, by virtue of being Balinese, views Barong and Rangda in this fashion. Among the people I interviewed in Bali, not all limited their observations to what they themselves perceived as individuals. A middle-aged male temple priest who began statements with the words "In Bali, we believe . . ." implied a unity of belief among all Balinese people that is only marginally less generalizing than the words of the foreign anthropologist. Such a statement can easily give rise to an essentializing one if I as the researcher report, based on the information from my contacts, that "the Balinese believe" this or that with respect to "their culture."

Hobart's further definition of culture as a construction is relevant here. Concepts of society and culture are "in no small part outsiders' [and these may come from as far away as another continent or as close as another village] constructions of an amalgam of processes, interpreted and disputed by those involved."[13] Both Rangda and the culture of which she is a part are changeable entities varying in accordance with time, place, and individual perception. In this book I endeavor to avoid essentializing Bali in the same way I avoid essentializing Rangda. That said, since many of my sources, especially the earlier secondary sources, do refer to "the Balinese" when indicating what the writer thinks to be majority views, I am compelled to use similarly general wording when citing these sources. I will, however, ask the reader to remember that generalizations, even those which have been widely accepted, are just that. The use of these more general statements in some portions of this book is tempered by those sections in which individuals with whom I spoke in Bali share their personal perceptions of Rangda.

Though my personal contacts were relatively small in number, they came from a variety of backgrounds. There were experts on Balinese religion and culture including the director of the largest art museum in the Peliatan/Ubud area, a school teacher in Tabanan, a *pemangku* (family or village priest, generally of the Sudra caste), a *pedanda* (Brahmin priest belonging to a higher caste than a *pemangku*) and a *balian* (traditional healer/magician belonging to a lower caste than a *pedanda*). In addition, I spoke with a couple running a homestay in Ubud, the female artist mentioned earlier who lived just outside of Ubud in Pengosekan, an American woman who had married a Balinese man and taken up residence in Peliatan, and some of the young women who made up the staff of one of the many internet cafés beginning to appear in the late 1990s around Ubud.

Introduction

Individual responses to the subject of my research were as diverse as the people themselves. Comfort levels when it came to speaking freely about Rangda in particular or about magic and witches in general also varied greatly: where some subjects seemed glad to explain their perception of Rangda to me, others displayed a marked reticence with this particular topic. The issue of witches or black magic is as a rule a sensitive one since is it difficult as a researcher to know the extent to which the individual being interviewed believes in black magic. A person who believes strongly may be afraid to discuss it from fear of repercussions, or he or she may simply not feel it a suitable topic to discuss with a stranger and a foreigner.

I mention this to point out that the language barrier is not the only significant obstacle faced when conducting research in Bali, or anywhere in the world outside of one's own culture group, for communication is a multi-step process depending not only upon grammar but also on the countless complex, culturally specific signifiers that imbues language with meaning beyond the words themselves. These may take the form of body language, the way in which words are chosen according to various contexts, the nature and length of the silences that punctuated speech, the avoidance of speech on certain topics, and so on. The discussion of these conceptual differences, as relevant to the topic of Rangda as she is encountered in Bali, forms the core part of this book.

Plate 1. *Barong I* by Hendra Gunawan (1974). Originally published in Agus Dermawan T. and Dr. Astri Wright *Hendra Gunawan: A Great Modern Indonesian Painter* (Singapore, Ir. Ciputra Foundation, 2001). Courtesy of the Ciputra Education Foundation

Plate 2. *Scene from a dramatic performance in which men who try to kill the witch-goddess Rangda turn their krisses on themselves under her spell* by Ida Bagus Made Togog (before 1942). Courtesy of Leo Haks

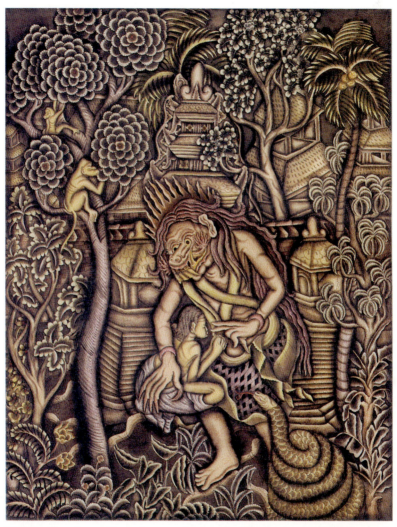

Plate 3. *Rangda, goddess of sorcery, bestows her blessing on a man meditating in her temple* by Ida Bagus Made Togog (before 1942). Courtesy of Leo Haks

Plate 4. *Dancer Stepping on My Head* by Kartika Affandi (1995). Courtesy of the artist

Chapter 1

Situating Rangda in Past Discourses

Agama Hindu Dharma, or Balinese Hinduism, is related to but not identical with the Hinduism found in India. It is built around a number of deities but dominated by a particular reverence for Siwa (known as Shiva in India). Though it may be described as a Siwaistic sect, Balinese Hinduism views Siwa not just as a single entity but as a vital part of the Trimurti, a trinity made up of Brahma, Siwa, and Wisnu (Vishnu). The power of the three gods of the Trimurti is then united in the form of Sanghyang Widi Wasa, the ultimate manifestation of the divine in Bali. The power of Sanghyang Widi Wasa can in turn be divided by two in the form of Rangda and Barong, by three as has been said, and so on to include all deities in the Balinese Hindu pantheon. Through this collapsing and expanding of identities, Balinese Hindu cosmology has the ability to take into account both the unified nature of the whole and the complexity of the parts that come together to form that whole.

Many aspects of Balinese Hinduism originated in India, including the names and basic natures of a number of the deities and the transmission of the myths that surround them. Bali was extensively Indianized by the late tenth century via the island's connection with Java, both through intermarriages among royal houses and through Javanese military action.[1] Despite this, the earlier animist tradition and ancestor worship practiced by the peoples of Bali was by no means wiped out, neither during this period nor later when Islam gained power in Java after the fall of the Majapahit Empire in 1515. Indeed, honoring the spirits of ancestors and a whole host of others is still a vital aspect of daily rituals and the absence of such attention would be seen as akin to neglecting to honor the gods, as these spirits have become one with the divine. Hinduism as a religion has the capacity to encompass many different things, including magical and Tantric practices. This flexibility facilitates the incorporation of the local practices of each new area adopting Hinduism. Thus, the strong belief in Bali in the prevalence and potency of magic is also a legacy of traditions existing on the island before the introduction of Hinduism. The legacy of magic as a force equally present in both left and right hand forms is thought to contain the roots of Bali's most powerful conduit of black magic, the figure of Rangda.

This background information has been accepted for some time by scholars of Bali as a basis for the understanding of Rangda, but in many cases it is also quickly abandoned as the discussion veers toward more European frames of reference. I refer in particular to an interest in the romantic and darker side of Balinese culture as it is seen to be embodied by Rangda and to the interpretation of the witch via psychoanalytic theory. The first has been most evident in the writings of Spies and Covarrubias, and the second in those by Mead and Belo.

Adrian Vickers wrote that "The Bali Hai (sic.) of *South Pacific* had nothing directly to do with the people who lived in Bali in the 1930s, but everything to do with Bali's image."[2] Here was a "Bali"—really a generic South Seas backdrop to a white romance—constructed by and for a foreign audience. This image was propagated not only in those books written with holiday-goers in mind, but is also evident from the 1930s output of the members of what Vickers called "the Bali circle." Walter Spies, Beryl de Zoete, Margaret Mead, Willem Stutterheim, and others were fascinated by both the island's loveliness and its people and by the darker side of paradise, with its witches and violent exorcism rites. The influence of Spies in propagating such images appears to have been considerable. His striking image of Rangda emerging from an eerie haze during a Barong performance has often been reprinted in books on Bali.

The scene from Spies and de Zoete's 1938 *Dance and Drama in Bali* epitomizes the construction of Rangda as an exotic denizen of darkness. The figures of three witches are foregrounded against a backdrop of palm trees rendered in silhouette by the mist and the rather theatrical quality of light. Brandishing magical white cloths, they approach the viewer with claw-like fingers outstretched. One can almost read demonic glee in the tilted back head of the central figure as she leers at the viewer. It is not entirely clear why more than one Rangda is shown. I am unaware of a performance of the Calonarang in which more than one dancer wears the mask of the witch, although it is not unusual for Rangda to appear with a number of her pupils. De Zoete and Spies did document an event in which several Rangda masks belonging to the same village were brought out to be worn by members of that village who fell into trance, possessed by the spirit of Rangda.[3] Although footage may possibly have been shot to document just such an event, Spies gives the impression of having been more interested in using the image as a means of conveying a sense of Rangda as he had come to understand her: the violent, monstrous, and supernatural witch; the maker of terrifying, inhuman cries capable of inducing a state of trance.

When I was in Ubud, the still image of this scene could be found in large quantities in the shops as cover art for a then-recent novel by Michael Weise entitled *On the Edge of a Dream: Magic and Madness in Bali*. Clearly Spies's Rangda has continued to be presented to tourists as a memorable image of the magical dark side of Bali. Early on in my stay, I Wayan Sugita, my assistant, suggested that I should read this book to help my understanding of Rangda. I asked him whether or not he had read it. It turned out that he had not, but had seen it in a shop. This conversation caused me to question my assumption that the material targeted at the tourist market was quite separate from material created for and by people living in Bali. When Wayan looked at the cover of Weise's book did he see an image of a Rangda he believed in, causing him to recommend that book to me as something he felt would be an accurate portrayal of her? Or did he identify the image and the book as something made purely for non-Balinese, therefore suggesting I pick up the book because I fit the profile of the target audience? It may be impossible to answer these questions, but what is clear is the way in which the legacy of the dark and the exotic from the 1930s has lingered on at the turn of the twenty-first century.

In the few studies from the early part of the twentieth century that dealt with Rangda in a less exoticizing way, the figure of the witch was primarily approached in terms of psychoanalytic theory. The following excerpt from Gregory Bateson and Margaret Mead's *Balinese Character: A Photographic Analysis* gives some idea of how Rangda was seen through this filter:

> While the Balinese child is passing through this first period of responding with passion to his mother's gay, disassociated teasing . . . he is also the spectator of the drama in which the Balinese express their feeling about just such a mother-role. The Witch-play, the Tjalonarang, the definitive dramatic theme of Balinese parent-child relations, not only expresses the residue in the adults of what they experienced as children, but also is watched by children and shapes their reading of the experiences to which they are subjected daily. It colors the child's appreciation of his mother's behavior, and stylizes his attitude toward her.[4]

The teasing Bateson and Mead refer to came from an instance in which they had witnessed a mother teasing her tiny son by twiddling his penis, an instance that Adrian Vickers has spoken of as one of the crucial moments in the couple's study of Bali. The frustrated child and the teasing mother are likened in this context to trance dancers attempting to confront the figure that constantly provokes them, only to render impotent their efforts to fight back with the small daggers they carry. The Barong is likened to a benevolent and protective father figure. To Jane Belo, Rangda was "a representation of the fear aspect of the Mother Figure."[5] This statement reinforces the notion that analysis such as this says more about the analyzer than the analyzed: we can draw from it that Belo was influenced by the psychoanalytic theories popular at the time she was writing.

"To be a good classical Freudian is to hold first, that all children entertain highly explicit sexual designs on at least one parent and murderous designs on the other, and, second, that the repression of those desires, even though it occurs in everyone, can bring on hysteria many years afterwards."[6] In the case of Rangda, however, both of these drives appear to have been placed upon the mother figure. Mead has written—and this was the one point on which Belo specifically disagreed with her—that Balinese men seek as sexual partners the archetype of the beautiful dancing girl, but that upon marriage, the girl would turn into Rangda in her relations with her husband. The man knows this will happen, but carries on nonetheless because he is unconsciously seeking someone who resembles his own mother.[7] In addition to being the parent to whom the male child is sexually attracted (female children are strangely not addressed outside of the idea that they will eventually become Rangda), the witch is also said to be the object of the child's murderous designs. Thus, acting out their repressed frustration toward their mothers, men who fall into trance during the dance performance will repeatedly attempt to stab the mother figure.

The use of Freud as the primary means of explaining Rangda is problematic on two levels. First, Mead's collapsing of the cross-gender aspects of the Oedipus complex and the erasing of Electra is unconvincing in terms of classical psychoanalytic theory. Secondly, I agree with Barbara Lovric's impression that "such theories seem anachronistic and inappropriate within the context of the culture, the myth and the morbidity. Obviously, there are many layers of meaning."[8] I do not want to take so strong a position with regards to psychoanalytic theory that I would approach this entire study as a critique of Freud, and in any case, that lies outside this study's framework. However, a discourse that has been conducted largely from this vantage point when there are so many other ways of approaching the material remains a problematic one. Any study that privileges one interpretation of Rangda to the exclusion of all others strikes me as inadequate for a full and rich exploration of the topic. In addition, if a single interpretation must be used, I find psychoanalytic

Situating Rangda in Past Discourses

theory to be a particularly inappropriate choice since, like Lovric, I see nothing in the cultural and social structure of Bali to support such an interpretation.

I have highlighted these two ways in which Rangda has been interpreted in the past because they have been the interpretations privileged by past writing that has dealt with the subject at any length. Subsequent writing, whether addressed to an academic or tourist audience, has tended to deal with Rangda very briefly. Tourist literature continues to sell "the exotic" with pamphlets featuring tag-lines such as "The Infamous Tale of Black Magic: Calonarang!!" used to advertise various spectacles arranged for the tourist market (in this case a nightly *wayang kulit* (shadow puppet) performance put on at a hotel in Ubud during the summer I was there).

Even when not so obviously composed for effect, the limited space that may be allotted to Rangda in the context of material written about Bali in general for tourists leads to much simplification of her character. One of the most truncated and one-dimensional descriptions I found was on a now defunct web page displaying a painting of Barong and Rangda by an unidentified artist that is set off with the caption "The Barong dance depicts the ever-present duel between Barong and Rangda—the forces of right and wrong." At the other end of the tourist spectrum, in an extensive description by tourist guide standards, she has been described as "the widow-witch Rangda—a manifestation of Siwa's consort. . . . She rules the evil spirits and witches who haunt the graveyards. Her world is darkness, and her specialties lie with the practice of black magic, the negative, destructive force of the left."[9]

Although this description fits well with the image of Rangda presented by Spies in his image of the three Rangdas emerging from the mist, it rings less true when we look at an image such as Hendra Gunawan's depiction of her in his 1974 painting *Barong I* (Plate 1). Rangda is shown as she might appear in a performance of the Calonarang, with the mask-like face, wild hair, and flaming tongue, but the palette Hendra uses to capture her features is hardly something tied to the world of darkness. Her costume is a riot of yellows, pinks, and oranges, and the veins zigzagging her breasts are magenta. She is shown dancing on a promontory high above a beach filled with throngs of Balinese in ceremonial dress.

Nearly a meter and a half tall, judging from the dimensions of the canvas, and placed emphatically in the foreground, the figure of Rangda seems oddly separate from the tiny, sketchy human figures in the distance. The contrast between the large-scale, highly worked image of Rangda and the more small-scale, loosely defined figures found in the rest of the painting serves to set her apart from the community, perhaps reflecting the way in which the darker forces that she has come to symbolize are so often viewed as something best kept at a distance. On the other hand, the strong colors that reverberate between fore and background draw the two elements back together and firmly establish Rangda as a participant in the human community's activities. This is reinforced by the painting's title, named not for the witch that dominates the picture plane, but for the sacred dance in which she and Barong do battle.

Here, although she may still be seen as a destructive force, the colors with which she is rendered (I have yet to see a Rangda mask that includes either pink or blue) make her less of a purely malevolent being than tourist literature would suggest. Hendra's palette makes her appear more grotesque than evil. Intentionally or unintentionally included on the part of the artist, the use of yellow in her hair and part of her costume could even be taken in accordance with traditional Balinese color symbolism to denote wisdom. Also, Rangda is shown facing away from the figures on the beach, aiming her demonic gaze and magical gestures elsewhere. As she does not menace the people involved in the ceremony, she seems more akin to Durga, destroyer of evil, than Kali, the barely controllable destroyer of all things. (Rangda's relationship with these two goddesses is discussed further in the next chapter.)

Scholarly writing has come to avoid exoticizing Rangda, but has done little to question the previous generation's psychoanalytic readings. Lansing has expressed some dissatisfaction with Belo's interpretation of Rangda as Fear itself, but after a single paragraph listing alternative readings suggested by his Balinese contacts (some the same as, some different from, readings proposed by my contacts), the reference is dropped, and the text reverts back to naming Rangda simply as "the personification of the evil powers in the universe."[10] Vickers has drawn question marks behind both the romanticism of Spies and the Freudian bias of Mead with regards to their approaches to the witch, but since Rangda was not the focus of his study, he did not follow through by proposing alternative interpretations. Part of my aim when I started my research was to pick up where Vickers left off.

The need to allow for more complexity than is generally found in discussions of Rangda starts even at the level of the background to her identity. Rangda cannot be categorized as simply a wicked witch. She is a historical figure from eleventh century Java, she is the villain in a play, she is a terrifying demonic figure found lurking around crossroads and graveyards, and she is an aspect of the consort of Siwa, who also takes the form of the young, pretty, and gentle rice goddess Dewi Sri. To people in contemporary Bali, as is clear from my interactions with individuals and from piecing together the multiple fragments of information in scholarly texts, she can be all of these things at once, taking on different aspects in different situations to fill a variety of agendas.

Chapter 2

Rangda's Singular Appearance and Multiple Identities

The question of Rangda's identity is a deceptively complicated one owing to the fact that it varies in accordance to context. Rangda is a title that refers to a historical figure, the villain in a play, and a goddess, roles that signal subtle changes in her nature. According to Lansing, she is also, along with Barong, arguably the most popular symbol among the Balinese.[1] Although it is hard to prove this high level of popularity in such an image-rich culture, it is safe to say that Rangda may be the most complex of Balinese symbols.

Sometimes shifts in nature may be signaled by changes in name, so that Rangda, Randeng Dirah, and Mahendradatta may all be used to refer to the same entity. Randeng Dirah is derived from the Balinese word *rangda* (literally, "widow") and the old East Javanese region of Dirah, hence, "the Widow of Dirah," the original Rangda. Mahendradatta is the name of the historical figure thought to have been the basis for the Rangda story.

As has been said, the word *rangda* is generally translated as "widow." This *rangda*, lacking a capital "R," does not refer to a specific individual but is a generic term. This is not to say that the two words are unrelated, for although the technical translation is "widow," the association with Rangda often leads to a translation as "witch" or even "widow-witch." When asked, some of the Balinese with whom I spoke would say that the word *rangda* means "widow," but the idea of sorcery, although often not directly and specifically linked, was rarely far off. Even after defining a *rangda* as a widow, they would go on to use the term interchangeably in reference to widows and witches. This is in all likelihood due to an association between a *rangda* and *the* Rangda, Queen of the Witches.

For example, Balinese artist Ida Bagus Nyoman Tjeta's *Balinese "Witches"* (Fig. 1), commissioned by Gregory Bateson and Margaret Mead in 1937, depicts a group of *rangda* worshipping Rangda their leader. Rangda is shown in the center,

7

Figure 1. *Balinese "Witches"* by Ida Bagus Nyoman Tjeta (1937). Originally published in Hildred Geertz, *Images of Power: Balinese Paintings Made for Gregory Bateson and Margaret Mead* (Honolulu: University of Hawaii Press, 1994). Courtesy of Hildred Geertz and the Bateson-Mead collection

with three heads to show the extent of her magical powers. Her followers, depicted as lesser versions of herself, gather round and pay homage. The spatial orientation of the figures on the picture plane is of lesser importance for my current discussion, as this stylistic element was often dictated to a greater or lesser extent by the tastes of visitors to Bali during the 1930s who were looking for depictions of exotic myths rendered in a pleasing decorative pattern. What the painting does help to illustrate, however, is the uses and associations of the word "R/rangda."

The painting's title, as well as the iconography, indicates that the smaller figures are *rangda*, that is to say, witches or sorcerers. The central figure to whom they defer is therefore Rangda, Queen of the Witches. Neither the title of the piece nor the accompanying text indicates that the figures depicted by the artist are intended to be widows. However, three of the Balinese I spoke with commenced their interview by telling me that *rangda* means "widow," and the glossary in Fred Eiseman's *Bali: Sekala and Niskala* gives that as the word's literal meaning. De Zoete and Spies have also explained that Rangda shares her name with the Balinese word for widow, "but to the idea of widow is attached a certain awe, even a degree of fear or horror. For a widow is the wife of a spirit and ought really to have given up her bodily form when her husband died, and to have followed him to the underworld."[2] I will not generalize to the extent of saying that all widows are thought to be witches or that all witches are thought to be widows, but I will suggest that the double-meaning is not lost on people in Bali. After all, Clifford Geertz noted in his study of the cockfight that the word for cock in Balinese produces the same *double entendre* as it does in English.[3] The Balinese are no strangers to puns.

In addition to the existence of the various roles that Rangda fulfills, aspects of her personality may change slightly from region to region, and even from village to village. As Lansing writes:

> One of the distinguishing features of Bali-Hindu . . . is that the gods are supposed to "blow like the wind" through Bali and alight from time to time at various temples. *It is only when resident at a temple that they have a personality.* Durga, for example, may be called Durga at temple X, and have a well-defined personality, but at temple Y three miles to the north she will have a different name and perfectly distinct personality when she comes to "visit."[4]

Presumably, both name and personality are determined by members of the priesthood who are thought to be in contact with the gods and can therefore transmit information about the nature of a deity and the name by which he or she wishes to be known to the people in the area. Although a survey of regional variations in the definition of Rangda's identity will not be undertaken here, this concept is relevant to the variety of individual opinions regarding the nature of the witch, as will be discussed in a later chapter. Rangda, like Durga of whom she is an aspect, will often mean different things to different people, even when her physical appearance remains much the same.

Iconography

Balinese or otherwise, most people who encounter Rangda experience her presence in visual form, particularly masks and stone sculpture. Distinctive iconography in the form of her bulging eyes, great fangs, long fiery tongue, and pendulous breasts make her easy to recognize. The use of visual conventions to aid members of a given culture in recognizing historical and religious figures is, of course, common in art around the world.

In general, the rules of representation for traditional Balinese art serve to distinguish between coarse and refined characters. The most refined characters have very delicate features as a physical extension of their pure and noble natures, while the coarsest are given highly exaggerated features—bulging eyes, large nose with flared nostrils, wide open mouth with oversized fang-like teeth—to demonstrate their rough manners and base impulses. This comes from what is often written of as a distinctive Balinese aesthetic that finds beauty in that which is small, delicate, and distinctively human and that can find cause for revulsion in that seen as more closely akin to the bestial.

Jane Belo has noted, for example, that the traditional punishment for incest required the offending couple to behave like animals for a set time.[5] This feeling is sufficiently strong for Balinese people to regard the human canine teeth, which are naturally slightly pointed, as too closely related to the animal world. One of the more important ceremonies for any individual involves the filing of these teeth, for it is felt that the person is susceptible to a dangerous level of passionate behavior (lust, anger, greed, arrogance, drunkenness, jealousy) until this has been done. It is unclear to what extent tooth-filing is currently practiced in urban areas where the effects of globalization have been felt more strongly, but I was aware of a number of non-Balinese acquaintances in Ubud who attended a tooth filing during my stay there. It was not spoken of as an uncommon occurrence.

As with the appearance of particular facial features, the colors used on the Rangda mask also help to describe her character. Many Rangda masks are painted white, but red masks may also be found both in tourist settings and in the context of sacred dance. In general, predominantly white masks often signal the character's purity, refinement, and noble birth, while red ones denote more dynamic, aggressive, or bestial qualities. Although research dealing with regional and individual variations among Rangda masks in particular has yet to be undertaken, it may be posited that white Rangda masks are meant to stress her royal birth, while red ones emphasize her violent nature.

In addition to the standard features denoting bad character, Rangda is given characteristics that allow her to be identified specifically as the Queen of the Witches. Rangda's canine teeth are not simply pointed but are exaggerated to the extent that they resemble tusks as would befit the supreme incarnation of the forces of darkness. From her gaping mouth protrudes a red and gold tongue of stylized flames that symbolizes her anger. Around her neck is a necklace of human entrails. She is shown with a mass of wild, coarse hair lacking in the hair ornaments usual to female figures but sometimes topped by flame that signals her great *sakti* or magical power. The large ear-plugs she wears indicate that she is female.

The way in which the body of Rangda is represented enhances this symbolism. Pendulous breasts mark her as an old woman, while claw-like fingernails and hairy knuckles suggest a bestial or demonic monstrousness to her character. Her tremendous personal power is enhanced by relative size—whether seen in sculptural form or as a costume worn as it traditionally is by a male dancer, she is presented as a large, impressive figure. These devices work together to create in the viewer the impression of an old woman who is as powerful as she is coarse, violent, and quick-tempered.

Although Rangda is most easily recognizable via her distinctive visage, it is not this so much as the black-and-white checked *poleng* cloth forming part of her costume that acts as the most effective symbol of what she means in Bali (Fig. 2). This cloth may be found wrapped around the waist of a dancer performing Rangda or around stone statues of Rangda at the time of a temple festival. The equal presence of the two opposites, black and white, symbolizes the presence of both the forces of left and right, of dark and light. Since it would be impossible for either to exist without the defining force of the other, the two together symbolize the dualities that make up the whole. Rangda's left hand magic is symbolized by the black squares and exists as an antithesis to the white that symbolizes the white magic power of her opponent, the Barong. Rangda's ability to be both a destructive and a protective force suggests that duality is also present within her. In either case, she is seen to function as a vital component of the totality of being.

Figure 2. Rangda wrapped in *poleng*

The appearance of Rangda is usually interpreted as above, with each physical characteristic taken as an outward manifestation of less tangible inner traits. Most of the literature on the subject either implies or states, as have I, that the iconography of Rangda is derived from conventions in Bali for the depiction of the demonic and the bestial.

Since the history of visual conventions relating specifically to Rangda is sketchy at best, it is difficult to state with assurance exactly where each element of her distinctive appearance comes from. Belo tentatively hypothesized that "the masked Rangda figure was elaborated out of the Durga worship belonging to the Sivaite tradition," but admitted a lack of supporting evidence capable of proving this with any sureness.[6] This uncertainty stands in contrast with the iconographic origin of the figure of the Barong (specifically, the Barong Ket), which is often hypothesized as derived from the form of a Chinese lion that, as in the Balinese version, functions to dispel evil. In the section of David Napier's *Masks, Transformation, and Paradox* dealing with Rangda and Barong, the various elements that make up the Barong's costume are dealt with in detail, while Rangda is mentioned more obliquely and generally in relation to the story of the Calonarang.[7]

Barbara Lovric's essay "Bali: Myth, Magic and Morbidity" proposes a different historically based source of the iconography that is also worth mentioning, as it provides an alternative to the usual interpretation by which Rangda's appearance is said to have developed from a long-running iconographic tradition for coarse or demonic characters. Lovric suggests that Rangda's attire of blood and entrails, rather than or in addition to being standard attributes of Indian tantrism and Kali worship, may be connected with the graveyard in a more literal than metaphorical sense.

She likens Rangda to a victim of plague, "the overwhelming hemorrhagic discoloration of the skin; the bulging, blood-shot, wide-open eyes; the protruding tongue and perforated abdomen associated with sudden death."[8] Like the mysterious stranger in Edgar Alan Poe's short story "The Masque of the Red Death," Rangda bears the appearance of a plague victim and functions as a symbol of pestilence. Since the figure of Rangda most often appears in the context of a sacred dance whose function is to ward off or rid a village of epidemic, it is plausible to link the very appearance of the witch with pestilence. In any case, this interpretation does not negate the more common interpretation that Rangda's appearance is the result of visual conventions of representation, nor does the latter explanation rule out the former. There is no reason why both could not be contributing factors to the representation of her physical form.

Rangda's Singular Appearance and Multiple Identities

Although the majority, if not all, written material in which Rangda is mentioned describes what she looks like as we currently know her, hypotheses of the process through which her appearance developed into this form are rare. In *Bali: Rangda and Barong*, Belo does not explicitly state a single historical point of origin for the iconography of Rangda as she appears today, but she does, following W. F. Stutterheim's 1930 *Oudeden von Bali*, track a number of stone carvings of Durga as she gradually comes to resemble the Balinese Rangda rather than the Indian Durga. The earliest of these dates to the tenth to thirteenth centuries and is located at Pura Kedarman in Koetri. Here, Durga is depicted as a supple and youthful beauty whose stance and proportions are not unlike sculptural forms found in India. A statue found in Bedoeloe from the thirteenth to fourteenth centuries shows a heavier, less voluptuous Durga with large canine teeth that Belo tentatively put forward as predecessors of Rangda's trademark tusks. The final statue is located in Pura Medoewe Karang, Koeboetambahan. Here, Belo followed not Stutterheim but C. J. Grader's 1940 study "De Poera Medoewe Karang te Koeboetambahan, een Nord-Balisch Agrarisch Heiligdon." This sculpture, although clearly meant to be Durga Mahisasuramardini (named for the episode in which the goddess slays the buffalo demon Mahisa) as evidenced by the placement of Mahisa under her upraised right foot, bears little resemblance to the Indianate lines of the Durga from Koetri. Instead, her appearance is strikingly similar to that of Rangda as she now appears in Balinese temple sculpture.

This gradual shift in the representation of Durga in Bali from the beautiful warrior goddess of India to the horrific witch Rangda could suggest that the iconography of Rangda developed along with the visual conventions that arose for the depiction of the darker forces in general as they appeared in masks, puppets, and stone sculpture. Alternately, one could say that from the tenth to the thirteenth centuries, the more purely Indianized influence of Hindu Java was strong in Bali and gave rise to a new interest in stone carving of a similar style. After the fourteenth century, however, contact with the now Muslim Java lessened considerably, causing Balinese sculptors to look increasingly to older indigenous shamanic forms and symbols.

I was interested in hearing the viewpoint of a *balian* on this matter, as part of his job involves being able to contact the spirits and to have a good working knowledge of both black and white magic. A discussion of the origins of Rangda in the home of a *balian* from the Tabanan area yielded a more specific explanation based upon Balinese religion:

> It's a long time ago, about eight generations before we could see Rangda and Barong as we do now. The Balinese people started with simple masks of Rangda and Barong

Iconography

using simple materials such as palm. People used palm leaves for the decoration of the Barong and the Rangda. And then one day, the spirit of the god came to the Rangda and the Barong. So that's the start of the Balinese people using Rangda and Barong as the symbol of good and evil . . .

With this interpretation, the iconography of Rangda is said to have come directly from the gods themselves, who instructed the Balinese people on the correct way to depict Rangda and Barong. The literature to date has not seriously explored a shamanic explanation such as this, where dreams and visions are presented as the source for innovation, as a viable interpretation. When it comes in the form of what Euro-North Americans might term as "myth," oral history relating to indigenous practices is still generally ignored in art history and much of anthropology as a serious explanation for the adoption and development of customs within a culture.

Whether derived from iconographic conventions that apply to much of traditional Balinese modes of representation, as a way of ritually resolving an occurrence of illness much too horrific to be dealt with in mere words, or as the dictate of god, the physical appearance of Rangda in contemporary times is consistent. I present this, of course, only as a relative consistency with the natural exception of subtle regional variations in traditional art throughout Bali. Occasionally, twentieth-century paintings made specifically with tourists in mind such as Ida Bagus Nyoman Tjeta's *Balinese "Witches"* will have modifications that may intend to take into account what are presumed to be non-Balinese tastes. In this painting, for example, Rangda's breasts are rendered much smaller and rounder than would normally be found. According to Hildred Geertz, this is done "in the spirit of tourist paintings,"[9] but one still cannot entirely rule out the possibility that the artist pursued this variation in accordance with his own vision of a *leyak*. Even with the existence of a certain number of variations in practice, in all of the literature on Bali, if Rangda makes even a brief appearance in the discourse via text or illustration, she is invariably described as I have described the traditional Rangda. In addition, any time I came across her in Bali, whether in stone, wood, or ink, or through the words of Balinese people I met, an image of this traditional Rangda was conjured up. Given this, one could safely surmise that whatever specific aspect of Rangda's complex nature a person may mean when they are speaking of her, this tends to be the image they have in their heads at the time.

That people envision Rangda in this fashion is clearly demonstrated in their descriptions of her, descriptions that are remarkably consistent regardless of whether they are speaking of a personal vision they once had or a masked dance performance watched as part of a crowd. Even a drawing of the Calonarang story by nine-year-old artist I Lungsur illustrated in Belo's essay "Balinese Children's Drawings" depicts Rangda in a manner remarkably similar to what has been described here. In summary, whether Rangda means the historical figure, the ferocious aspect of a local village *leyak*, or an aspect of Dewi Durga, the outward form remains very much the same.

With Rangda's physical form described, the next section surveys the different personages that can be meant when she is referred to. This will begin with the story of the historical Rangda and some of the most common variations thereof, then move on to the Rangda found in dance-drama as observed throughout the twentieth century, followed by a description of Rangda as part of the Hindu Balinese pantheon.

Rangda as a Historical Figure

The original Rangda is said to have lived in East Java during the eleventh century. Her name is given by historians and anthropologists as Mahendradatta, a Javanese princess whose son was King Erlangga (also Airlangga), a historical figure known to have assumed the throne on Java in the year 1019 CE. My conversations with a number of Balinese, some high-caste and well-educated ones among them, suggest that this name is perhaps not so well known or widely used in current day Bali as it would appear from its regular inclusion in anthropological studies. Other names from the same story did appear in various interviews, such as Erlangga, Ratna Mengali, and Mpu Baradah (also Empu Pradah), but none of the subjects mentioned Mahendradatta. Many people refer to the historical figure instead as either Calonarang or Randeng Dirah.

Regardless of the name used, the basic elements of the story are much the same. Upon learning that Mahendradatta practiced black magic, her husband banished her to the forest and took another wife. The subsequent death of the king—some say by his exiled wife's magic—left Mahendradatta a widow. Although there existed a growing rift with her son Erlangga, whom she blamed for failing to take her side when she was exiled, the thing that angered Mahendradatta most was that now nobody was willing to marry her daughter.

Mahendradatta's daughter, Ratna Mengali, does not appear in art nearly as frequently as her mother, but when she is shown it is as a young woman of great beauty. Covarrubias included an image of her from an unidentified Balinese manuscript in his *Island of Bali*, where she appears with a sarong wrapped around her slender waist and delicate ornaments in her hair. In form and attire, the image is not dissimilar to images of Sita, the beautiful and good heroine of the *Ramayana*.

In the story it was widely known that Ratna Mengali was beautiful, but it was also widely known that her mother was a terrible witch. Since the thought of having a witch for a mother-in-law was a sufficiently unattractive proposition to outweigh the benefits of having a lovely princess for a wife, the young woman was unable to find a husband. Enraged at the thought of her daughter's being shunned, Mahendradatta, who at this point in the story begins to be called Rangda, used her magic to unleash an epidemic. Erlangga, now king, feared for his people and realized that decisive action was necessary. Although he did not initially know for certain the reason behind the sickness, a meeting with his chief advisors soon revealed the cause to be the angry widow. It was known to the king's advisors that Rangda got her power from a *lontar*, a magic book made up of text scratched onto palm leaves, so they contrived a plot in which the prime minister's son would marry Ratna Mengali and steal the book. Unfortunately for them, Rangda's magic allowed her to foresee what was being planned and she flew into an even greater rage at the attempted trick. She immediately responded with another, more devastating epidemic.

Since Rangda's magic was obviously too strong for the government to deal with, the King asked for the help of a holy man named Mpu Baradah. The priest had a thorough knowledge of white magic but none of black magic, so it was still necessary for him to obtain Rangda's *lontar* in order for him to learn black magic so that he could effectively do battle with the witch. To this end, he enlisted the help of his assistant, Bahula, and launched a plot similar to that which had been attempted by the prime minister's son. Whether due to the holy man's superior wisdom or simple luck, the plot was successful this time, and Mpu Baradah was brought the *lontar* from which he immediately began teaching himself black magic. Armed with his new knowledge, he was able to challenge Rangda to a sorcerer's duel. Rangda, now appearing in her recognizable, ferocious form, used her magic to set a large Banyan tree aflame and surround her opponent with a ring of fire. Protected by his own magic, Mpu Baradah was unharmed by the flames. He first restored the tree to show his strength, and then killed Rangda, first in her monstrous form and then again when she returned to human form.

This version of the story of Rangda is based on that recorded by R. Ng. Poerbatjaraka. Details vary depending upon the region in which the story is told and on the individual recounting it, but I have chosen to include this version as it is that most commonly cited in studies of Rangda.

Rangda's Singular Appearance and Multiple Identities

Rangda is generally said to have been a high caste woman from the East Javanese province of Dirah (sometimes spelled Girah) during the eleventh century reign of King Erlangga, but her exact relationship to the royal court is unclear. In some versions, as with that given above, she is a close relative of the ruler; in others she is given no named relatives save for her daughter. Needless to say, whether or not Rangda is the mother of the king whose mortal enemy she becomes has a strong impact on the way in which one interprets the story, but more on this later. Being such a vital motivating factor for Rangda's behavior, the daughter is naturally always present, but the question of her paternity is so infrequently dealt with that one is made to wonder if it is known. In the story as it has been presented here, the reader may assume that Ratna Mengali's father is the same as Erlangga's, that is to say Mahendradatta's husband, the King. Even when he is not mentioned directly, the fact that Rangda is a widow alludes to a former husband and likely father of one or both of her children. The story increases in complexity when a quite different paternity is proposed, as was the case in an interview with the *pemangku* who said that Ratna Mengali had no mortal father and her mother had made her using a flower.

Another detail to do with Rangda's daughter, one sometimes included and sometimes omitted, is her complicity in her mother's destructive use of black magic. Often Ratna Mengali risks being condemned to perpetual spinsterhood, itself frowned upon by the society in which she lived, simply due to her mother's magical practices. In many versions of the tale, however, the daughter is explicitly implicated in the mother's actions. There is often a segment of the story that tells of Ratna Mengali's being sent along with a group of young women referred to as Rangda's pupils to the graveyard where they must find the corpse of a baby for a black magic spell. This detail appears often enough that its omission could be interpreted as a decision made due to space and time restrictions when telling the story rather than to any ambiguity in the teller's mind regarding Ratna Mengali's intentions in following her mother's career path.

Like legends in my own culture, the story of the angry widow and her fight with Mpu Baradah is so well known to so many people in Bali that it need not always be told in its entirety, as the audience is capable of filling in the missing elements. This said, one must not forget that the texts in which the narrative segment about Ratna Mengali appears tend to be written down by non-Balinese authors drawing on R. Ng. Poerbatjaraka's version of the story. This version of the Calonarang has become the norm through repetition in the works of Euro-North American writers, and as such should not be seen as something that categorically rules out other levels of ambiguity and diversity possible in the way the story may be told in Bali.

Rangda in Sacred Dance

The story of the historical Rangda forms the basis of the Calonarang dance-drama, the present form of which is thought to have originated in about 1890 in the southern Balinese region of Gianyar. Dance-drama in general refers to a popular form of Balinese performance art in which stories are transmitted to the community through dance. Elaborately costumed dancers, sometimes masked and sometimes not, act out the narrative through a combination of spoken word and stylized movement. Many of these stories are, like the Calonarang, based on tales from the royal houses of East Java elaborated during the eleventh to thirteenth centuries. As has been said, the Calonarang dance follows the basic outline of the story of Rangda related above. This is with one notable exception: as a performance piece, the Calonarang invariably includes Rangda's fight with the Barong, a fight that lacks a permanent resolution of the conflict between the opposing forces.

Most famously appearing in the form of a creature that closely quite resembles a Chinese lion, the Barong is a mythical creature symbolic of white magic and the forces of good, basically the antithesis of Rangda. The point at which Barong came to be associated with the historical story of Rangda is unclear, especially as different productions of the Calonarang will introduce Barong in different ways. The timing is the same, occurring after Mpu Baradah's duel with the witch (and in this case he is unable to kill her), but in some versions the holy man transforms himself into Barong to defeat Rangda, while in others Barong is an individual entity that takes the side of Mpu Baradah in the fight with the witch.

There appears to be a certain amount of flexibility here, as the struggle between Rangda and Barong is viewed to some extent as a story in itself that may be inserted into the framework of other narratives as appropriate for the occasion of the performance. The precise extent of this flexibility is difficult to isolate, as my first-hand experience of seeing the fight between Barong and Rangda occurring outside the context of the Calonarang is limited to tourist performances. In the *wayang kulit* show I observed in Ubud, the performance consisted of a telling of the Mahabharata epic that blended into the story of Rangda's fight with Barong.

The introduction of the Barong is one departure from the traditional narrative surrounding the historical Rangda, but the manner of the witch's defeat in the dance-drama presents a far greater change. Namely, Rangda never dies in the Calonarang dance. The usual ending for the story of the historical Rangda in which Mpu Baradah twice kills Rangda is nicely summarized by Colin McPhee, working with a translation from Old Javanese by R. Ng. Poerbatjaraka: "In a fury she reproaches him for reanimating her. The holy one replies that this was done in order to give her a last opportunity for repentance. And so the *rangda* is calmed, and, having been taught the way of redemption, is killed once more, in a state of absolution."[10]

In dance performances, by contrast, Rangda is not killed, but only made to flee. In the first version of the tale, Rangda is neutralized and destroyed, thus permanently removing her potential to do evil. In the second, she is only repelled, with the implication that she may come back again at any time. Here, evil is not eradicated but only pushed a little further away from oneself and the community. Since this difference signals a shift between the way evil is conceived of and dealt with, it also signals a shift in the construction of Rangda as a symbol of evil.

Rangda and Karma

The double killing of Rangda in the oral tradition as a means of facilitating her atonement for her crimes could conceivably be linked to the Hindu belief in karma and its effect of reincarnation, although the differences between what could be called orthodox Hinduism and Balinese Hinduism invariably make such comparisons problematic. If a person's fate in this life has been cosmically predetermined in accordance with actions in the previous life, then actions in this life will in turn have a direct impact on the quality of the next life. Positive and negative acts accumulate good and bad karma. According to this model, Rangda's predilection toward spreading epidemics would have caused her to accumulate an extraordinarily large amount of bad karma, likely to result in her reincarnation as a low caste human or, worse, an animal or demonic being. In addition, before this reincarnation occurred, she would be forced to undergo a period of torment in hell.

A work in pen and ink, watercolor, and crayon done between 1928 and 1942 by an anonymous Balinese artist illustrates the idea of torment arising from the accumulation of bad karma. Scenes of punishments to the soul occurring after the death of the body are common in Balinese painting and relief sculpture. The descriptive title accompanying the image as it appears in *Pre-War Balinese Modernists 1928–1942: An Additional Page in Art History* reads: *'Tjerita Derman' A woman, possibly Sri Tanjung, travels to purgatory. On her path are Sang Suratma, scribe of sins, and Sang Jogormanik, who dictates punishments* (Fig. 3). The reader should be cautious when confronted with words such as "sin" and "purgatory" of interpreting these in the context of Christian tradition. Such words are often used, as indeed they are here, because they are the closest available translations for a similar but by no means identical concept found in another culture.

Figure 3. *"Tjerita Derman"* *A woman, possibly Sri Tanjung, travels to purgatory. On her path are Sang Suratma, scribe of sins, and Sang Jogormanik, who dictates punishments* by an unknown painter (before 1942). Courtesy of Leo Haks

Tjerita Derman depicts a woman traveling to purgatory, passing on the way Sang Suratma and Sang Jogormanik. Both figures are shown as demonic forms (as indicated by their bulging eyes, pointed teeth, and beast-like noses), making them suitable for the administration of hell. On either side of the path are men and women undergoing various forms of torture meted out by Sang Jogormanik, with different torments corresponding to different sins committed during life. For example, the tree on the left bank from which daggers fall is called "the Tree of Suspicion." A painting such as this may be taken as further evidence of a Balinese concern with the consequences of one's actions during life as is shown by the fearful expressions of the four men who approach the demonic figures ready to hold them to account for the bad karma that they have accumulated.

In reviving Rangda and causing her to see the error of her ways (in other words, bringing about an awakening of conscience), Mpu Baradah is able to help her offset, even if only by a minute measure, the large sum of bad karma that would condemn her to misery in the next life. This is the reading suggested by McPhee and others, with the idea that Rangda was killed once and then revived so that she might die "in a state of absolution." No one appears to have questioned why she must be killed at all if she has, indeed, been made to see the light. Perhaps it is thought that she must forfeit this life in order to be granted a chance of improvement in the next.

Through her death, the Rangda in this story is made an example. She is shown to be wicked, and by repenting her past behavior after her total defeat she acknowledges that she has been in the wrong and that society's norms are right. When I asked a *pemangku* to sum up Rangda in a few words, he said she is synonymous with "bad character." As a powerful villain who repents before dying, the Rangda in this story capitulates to the side of right and good in the form of Mpu Baradah, and through this act reinforces the culture's social mores.

When Rangda gleefully runs off at the end of the Calonarang dance, the implication is that she is not being made an example in the same way. In performance art, Rangda is not a simple symbol of negative behavior, but a symbol of the balance that is so important to Balinese Hinduism. Balinese cosmology is written of as envisioning all things divided into pairs: good and evil, day and night, life and death, white magic and black magic, male and female, the mountains and the sea, and so on through all things in the world. Both components of each duality are accepted, and the drama lies in the negotiations between the two. Although certain things may be more desirable than others—good is more pleasant than evil, clean is generally better than unclean—all are necessary and part of the natural order of things. Therefore, while the Barong symbolizes white magic and positive forces and Rangda black magic and negative forces, it is not expected that good can permanently conquer evil. This could be viewed as an example of Bali Hindu realism, based upon an empirical observation of history and human nature.

The On-going Battle between Rangda and Barong

The theme or moral of the story in dance form is not the eradication of the forces of evil and the triumph of good, but instead achieving balance and harmony between the two elements.

To illustrate just how this works, I will summarize the action during the portion of the dance-drama that deals with the fight between Barong and Rangda. Barong enters the dance stage first, playfully snapping its jaws at the audience seated around three sides of the rectangular enclosure. As the iconography of the mask suggests—bulging eyes, large fangs, and so forth—the Barong looks like a monster but is, in fact, a good spirit that holds the welfare of the village at heart. After a short gamboling dance by the Barong followed by his retiring into one corner of the clearing, a strange shriek offstage and/or the appearance of long fingernails from around a door-frame mark the entrance of Rangda.

The witch prowls around flicking a magic white cloth and occasionally calling out phrases in the Old Javanese language of *Kawi*. An archaic, literary language spoken by the high-born characters in dance-dramas and puppet performances, *Kawi* is unintelligible to most Balinese, who need it interpreted for them when it is used in dance. *Kawi* is also a highly potent tongue, both in spoken and written form and, especially so, in the written form used in the writing of magical texts on *lontars*.

Although Rangda's primary target is Barong as the protector of the village, she does not attack him directly. Instead, she uses the spell of her magic cloth to induce a state of trance in his followers. These men attempt to attack her with their daggers, but her magic causes them to turn their blades upon themselves. This can be seen in a painting by Ida Bagus Made Togog descriptively titled *Scene from a dramatic performance in which men who try to kill the witch-goddess Rangda turn their krisses on themselves under her spell* (Plate 2). Rangda dwarfs the two men who clamber up her body as she dances, trying to stab her and failing as her power bends their blades. Two more would-be attackers have already fallen to the ground under the influence of her magic.

If one thinks of this short sequence as a battle in itself, Rangda has won. However, Barong's white magic is just as strong as Rangda's black magic, and its protective power prevents the trance dancers from harming themselves with their daggers. The Barong's beard dipped in holy water provides an antidote to the black magic induced trance, and Rangda, seeing how she has been thwarted, decides to retreat and bide her time until the next encounter. So, although Barong is sometimes said to have won the fight against Rangda, this is not strictly true in the sense of winning outright. Barong succeeds in frustrating the witch's attempt to wreak havoc in the village, but one is not meant to get a sense of the triumph of good. It could be said that the fight results in a draw, having no real winner. In repelling Rangda, Barong has simply restored balance. When stated in this fashion, the reader may be led to think that little has been accomplished, but that would be wrong. Maintaining balance is so central both to Balinese cosmology and to daily life that few things could be seen as more important than its preservation.

Interpreting Rangda's flight from the dance stage at the end of the performance as a form of banishment, it may be tempting to think that Barong has won a decisive victory after all. This is based on the notion that for many in Bali, banishment from the community is considered a fate far worse than death, as it is thought to disorient the soul and disrupt the cycle of reincarnation. In this light, Barong's ability to put Rangda to flight is, in fact, a greater punishment than the death of Mahendradatta at the hands of Mpu Baradah. However, it should be remembered that the ending of the Barong and Rangda dance is always a somewhat open one, in that it is generally understood that Rangda has not run away very far or for very long. She is effectively not banished at all.

The idea of there not being a decisive victory for one side or the other is important to the Balinese conception of the dualities that pervade all aspects of existence. For Barong and the side of good to win the fight would be just as disastrous to balance as it would be for Rangda and the side of evil to win. In the story of the historical Rangda on which the dance-drama is based, there is a clear victory for Mpu Baradah as the representative of good. The implication of this ending, that the forces of darkness can and should be vanquished, runs counter to the symbolism apparent in the much more open ending of the Calonarang dance.

There are several possible explanations for this. To begin with, there is the link to the orthodox Hinduism that was proposed earlier with regards to the problematic issue of karma as it pertains to Hinduism in Bali. Although Balinese Hinduism includes a belief in reincarnation, the fact that none of my contacts in Bali spoke of it suggests that there may be a less direct reference to karma than one finds in India. This is not to say that people in Bali categorically do not believe in or give consideration to the concept of karma, merely that the individuals I spoke with did not appear to concentrate on it to the same degree. This is due in large part to the incorporation of local ancestor worship into the Hindu philosophy imported from India.[11] It is believed that when a Balinese person dies, he or she will be reincarnated as a member of the same family. It is unclear at what point exactly the relationship between the orthodox and Balinese Hindu parameters set for reincarnation was worked out, and therefore how it relates to the eleventh-century morality of Rangda is unclear. It is possible, however, that at the point when the story of Mahendradatta first began to be told there was a closer link to the Indian conception of karma and reincarnation, and the narrative thus had an element of this built into it.

A more likely reason for the difference relates simply to function. When transmitted as a story, either orally or in manuscript or pictorial form, a central purpose of Mahendradatta's tale is didactic. The closed ending in which Mahendradatta is clearly defeated indicates that behavior such as hers is not condoned by society. The story functions to indicate to those who hear it the type of passionate and uncontrolled behavior that will not be tolerated by that society. The Calonarang dance, however, is not only a retelling of a famous story, but a sacred ritual. Rangda does not cease to be constructed as a negative behavioral example here, but this function is secondary to maintaining a balance between the forces of left and right. Ceremonial dances such as that featuring the fight between Barong and Rangda serve not only to transmit moral lessons and histories to the populace but also to act as offerings to the gods, as rituals of purification, and, at times, as exorcism rites.

Although ceremonial dances rarely belong in one category to the exclusion of all others, the Calonarang could be said to fit best into the category of exorcism rites. This naturally excludes tourist performances that, although following the outward form of the ceremonial dance, have no intrinsic ritual value. The Calonarang dance in its ritual form is usually held when there is sickness in a village and with the express purpose of appeasing or banishing the powers that caused it. In Bali, sickness has traditionally been seen to be caused not by germs, but by black magic, either from ill-tempered local *leyak* or from spirits who feel they have been neglected. To remedy an illness, therefore, it is necessary to fight back with magic. Magic is definitely at work in the Calonarang, as dancers do not simply act out the story of Rangda and Barong, but actually become possessed by the spirits of the characters they are dancing. The struggle between Barong and Rangda in dance form is not exclusively a reenactment of the story, as the forces of good and evil are really doing battle through the conduit of the human dancers.

The Potency of the Rangda Mask

In the sacred dance as it is performed today, the Rangda we see is not simply a character called Mahendradatta or Randeng Dirah, and not exactly just a dancer in a costume, but the larger-than-life figure of the mythological Queen of the Witches, a powerful spirit, a goddess. In Balinese cosmology, Rangda is no less real in this context than she is when viewed exclusively as a historical figure. The story's didactic aspects are pushed into the background because the black magic that causes illness in the village is now fighting with the white magic that protects the village. Black magic must be subdued in order to bring people back to health, but should never be destroyed altogether as this would upset the forces and bring chaos. In dance, therefore, Rangda is a symbol of negative forces that are a necessary part of balance. Here Rangda is powerful in a real sense: she is a malevolent spirit that will spread destruction if allowed to proceed unchecked, and yet by acting as a counterpoint to the white magic of Barong, she also preserves balance.

In order to make clearer how the spirit of Rangda can be present in the form of a masked dancer, I will briefly outline the key steps in the making of a sacred mask. The carvers of sacred masks tend to come from carving families and must undergo purification rites before beginning their carving careers. To begin a Rangda mask, a small amount of wood is taken from a living tree, seen as a sacred tree whose permission must be sought by the carver and a priest through prayers and offerings at the time of the cutting. The wood is taken to the village temple, where it is stored until it has sufficiently dried out and an auspicious date has been determined. Before carving can begin, offerings must be made and holy water sprinkled on the wood and the carving tools. Carving and painting take place in the temple, after which a purification ceremony is held basically to apologize to the mask for having been placed on the floor, stepped over, and subjected to other treatment considered to be demeaning for a sacred object.[12]

In the final and most important ceremony, the spirit of Rangda is invited to enter the mask made in her image. This is done at night with the whole village present. If the ceremony is successful, it is said that the deity will enter the mouth of the mask in the form of a ball of fire. The mask is then considered to be *tenget*, imbued with the supernatural power of Sanghyang Widi Wasa, the one entity in which all deities, including Rangda, are ultimately unified. From this point on, the mask is treated with respect as an esteemed member of the community and one that will act as a protector of the village for as long as it continues to be cared for appropriately. In order to maintain the good-will of the deity, offerings are made to the mask on specific days as well as every time it is used in sacred dance. No one who is ritually impure may touch the mask, and severe illness has been known to result from a person looking through a Rangda mask without having first undergone the proper purification rituals.

Rangda in the Temple

Rangda's power and influence are not limited to sacred dance, but extend far beyond into the lives of many Bali Hindus in her capacity as a deity. Her outward appearance is the same as has been described, but the medium is changed to fit the context. This Rangda most frequently appears in the form of temple sculpture, particularly in the Pura Dalem, or temple of death, one of the three primary temples found in every community. The Pura Dalem is dedicated to Siwa the Destroyer and to his consort Durga.

Although Rangda the goddess is not totally divorced from the historical figure Randeng Dirah, the Balinese with whom I spoke did not think of the two as entirely interchangeable either. When asked about Rangda, they often related the story of Mpu Baradah and the angry widow, but they made a distinction between the character in the story and the Rangda found in the temple. As I Ketut Arthana, a *pedanda* from the Marga area told me, "Rangda does not always have a bad character. The bad character, that is just in the story." Mask maker Ida Bagus Sutarja described Rangda to Michele Stephen, author of *Desire, Divine and Demonic*, as the "Mother" and that ". . . to kill her would be to destroy the very source of our own being."[13] Thus, the Rangda one might meet in the graveyard has a subtly different nature than the character in the legend.

These shifts in the objective "truth" of Rangda's identity are similar to those signaled by Belo in her discussion of the association between Rangda and Durga. Although it could be said that Rangda indeed *is* Durga, she is no more identical to Durga than the Black Christ of the Aztecs is to Jesus of Nazareth.[14] Or, to continue with my analogies to popular culture, compare the various perceptions of the relative reality of any of Rangda's identities to the relationship between a film actress and a popular role she has played. To some viewers, the fictional character she has portrayed is clearly different than the actress "in real life." For other viewers, the identity of the actress as a person may be blurred with or even lost in favor of the characteristics of the fictional character.

The Pura Dalem in any given village is appropriately located next to the cemetery. To enter the Pura Dalem in Ubud, one must first ascend a flight of moss-covered stone steps decorated at intervals with demonic stone figures and skull forms. Presiding at the top of the steps is a slightly over life-size figure of Rangda (Fig. 4). She leers at the viewer, casually resting one foot upon a skull and holding a child's corpse. Anyone wishing to enter the temple proper must pass directly under this figure's watchful eyes. Smaller statues of Rangda are found here as well, and also on the boundaries of the graveyard itself (Fig. 5). Wherever these statues may be found, Rangda (or a *leyak* advanced enough to appear in her image) is shown as a terrifying figure, open-mouthed in preparation to feed upon the infant corpses that further fuel her great *sakti*.

It is important to note that Rangda is in no way relegated to the distant past as a purely legendary figure. True, her background is still linked with the story of the historical figure Mahendradatta, as is evidenced by the fact that a number of the people I spoke with, namely the *pemangku*, the school teacher from Tabanan, A. A. G. Dela Aribuana (known to the guests of his homestay Pak Agung after the name of the establishment) and Agung Rai (director of ARMA, the Agung Rai Museum of Art), gave a summary of this story when asked about Rangda. Despite this, these same individuals did not appear to accept her death, or at least not in such a way that would prevent her from also being alive and well in the context of temple ceremonies. This view is echoed by the short description of Rangda in Hobart, Leeman, and Ramseyer's *The Peoples of Bali*, which says that the Supreme Witch is "confronted, but never defeated" by the Barong,[15] and in Belo's *Bali: Rangda and Barong*, which states how "over and over, the Balinese reiterate . . . 'you cannot kill her.'"[16] She is therefore given a set of characteristics, not dependent upon the eleventh-century myth, that describe her nature and current presence in the village. In her association with the Pura Dalem, Rangda rules over the forces of death and destruction. This is where here role as the mistress of black magic comes to the fore.

According to much if not all of the literature on Bali, the Balinese have always believed strongly in the presence and power of magic on the island, a sentiment that, as my own research suggests, carries through to the present day. For example, the artist Murni explained how it was possible to identify a person who practiced black magic by looking into his or her pupils and seeing the image of Rangda there. Armed with this knowledge, one would then avoid any further eye contact to prevent the person from attacking with his or her magic. In this context, Rangda is not so much the incarnation of evil as she is the face of black magic power.

Humans who wish to attack others with magic or to prevent similar attacks on them by others will go to the Pura Dalem and pray to Rangda for her assistance. If approached with proper ceremony, Rangda will answer their prayers for good or ill.

Figure 4. Rangda, Ubud Pura Dalem

Figure 5. Rangda, Peliatan cemetery

In a painting by Ida Bagus Made Togog, done between 1928 and 1942, the descriptive title tells us that here *Rangda, Goddess of Sorcery, bestows her blessing on a man meditating in her temple* (Plate 3). In this scene Rangda does not behave in the violent, uncontrolled manner of the witch in the story, but as a goddess rewarding one who has honored her with the gift of magical power. Her right hand displays the characteristic claw-like fingernails, but they are shown as doing no harm to the figure of the meditating devotee encircled by her protective arm. As Agung Rai told me, "If you are nice to Rangda, Rangda will be nice to you."

When picturing the Rangda to whom one may pray in the temple, her physical presence is, again, the same as has been described. Her behavior, however, is not dependent upon the demands of a narrative in which she fulfills the role of the villain, the negative element in the story. She is constructed here as the quintessential *leyak*, as is in keeping with her position as the queen of black magic power. Her favorite haunt is the graveyard, especially after dark. This is appropriate for a *leyak*, as it is known to many if not most Balinese that the best way to attain the ability to do black magic is to undergo nocturnal meditations in the local graveyard. This is something anyone can attempt. If he or she has exceptionally good strength of mind, the power will come, granted by the gods. Since Rangda is the ruler over such powers, she tends to be envisioned as the stereotypical *leyak*, that is to say, she spends time in the cemetery, devours babies, and revels in magically causing illness and general bad luck.

The iconography of her statues reflects this, as examples from Ubud and Peliatan show. In her capacity as a deity, however, such actions are given a specific function. In Bali, as has been said, personal misfortunes may be caused by black magic, either at the hands of local *leyak* or by the power of Rangda herself. It is also thought that such things only befall those people who have somehow transgressed Hindu practice and accumulated bad karma.[17] If an individual does not make the proper offerings to the gods, that person places himself or herself greatly at risk of attack by black magic. Rangda will only disturb people who in some way fail to honor the gods. In this way, she acts as a deity working on behalf of all other deities to punish the unfaithful. Thus, through her attacks by black magic, Rangda ultimately serves the mechanisms of justice and truth. (The concept of Rangda as a potential agent of good is further discussed in Chapter 3.)

Rangda's Terrible Power Today

Do people in present-day Bali fear Rangda? Do they believe in her as the very real and potent being described here thus far? These were questions I often found myself asking as I endeavored to find out just what Rangda meant in the context of Bali at the time I was there.

Writing on the subject of sorcery in 1980, C. Hooykaas noted that though belief in *leyak* in general was still widespread, the number of skeptics was growing.[18] According to the high school teacher from Tabanan whom I interviewed, Rangda has lost much of her power to terrify in recent years because of advances in technology and inroads made into the culture by the Western scientific viewpoint. This teacher was introduced to me by my assistant, Wayan, who had been one of his students some years before. The interview took place at the home of Wayan's cousin just outside the town of Tabanan. The family's living space is built onto the back of a mechanic's garage that they run. The teacher had the following to say about Rangda's currency:

> Now, every place has electricity, so it's not like before. When there was no electricity, it was very dark in the villages, so children were more easily scared by the Rangda story. But now, it's different. The children aren't very scared of Rangda because they want to know the reality. They don't believe. They hear it as a story, but they want to know the reality.

As for adults, it was his feeling that about half the Balinese now believe in Rangda's magic. I later posed the question to Agung Rai, asking him whether all people in Bali were scared of Rangda. After making a distinction between Calonarang performances put on for tourists and sacred rights in which Rangda appears, he indicated that in the latter context, Rangda is, indeed, universally feared even today.

Of the Balinese men and women I interviewed at length, the two who made a point of saying that Rangda frightened them personally were Ibu Agung, as I came to know the wife of A. A. G. Dela Aribuana, the owner of the homestay where I lived while in Ubud, and Murni the painter. Ibu Agung, like many people in Bali, had first been introduced to Rangda in through dance performances when she was a child. She described seeing the figure of Rangda and then coming home after the performance where she had nightmares caused by the terrible face of the witch and the powerful magic of which she was capable. She soon decided that when Rangda appeared, it was best not to look, a tactic she continues to employ. For Murni, Rangda was terrifying in a real and tangible way. She described coming home from the movies after dark, encountering on the way the image of Rangda, complete with big round eyes and long tongue. This experience, which, she stressed, had not been a dream, frightened her so much that she became reluctant to venture out by herself at night. When I asked her whether she thought all people were scared of Rangda in this fashion she said no. Still, this did not prevent her from telling her non-Balinese boyfriend point blank that he was crazy for saying that if he ever saw Rangda he would try to get a good look at her face, and perhaps even snap a photograph of her.

More recently, Kristi Ross's 2003 article in *Parabola* describes a Rangda that is as relevant and as powerful as ever, stating that "No Balinese doubts Rangda's powers."[19] Whether all Balinese, children and adults alike, treat Rangda with the mixture of fear and awe that Ross suggests is unknowable as it ever was. That said, if the *leyaks* who follow Rangda have managed to add motorbikes, driverless cars, and airplanes to their modern repertoire of transformation, then the Queen of the Witches herself cannot be too easily relegated to the past tense.

Rangda as an Aspect of Durga or Kali

Thus far when I have spoken of Rangda as a goddess or deity, it has been in a rather vague way that made little attempt to outline where such a being would fit in the Hindu pantheon. Indeed, it is a difficult issue, as the Balinese did not indiscriminately import every single god and goddess when they adopted Hinduism, omitting some and adding others. This makes a good deal of sense, as polytheistic religions generally have some regionally specific deities in their pantheon that are well-suited to the physical or emotional landscape of one area and not another. I use the term "polytheistic" quite loosely here and purely in the sense that the Balinese use many names to address the divine. If asked, many Balinese would likely say that their religion is monotheistic, as all of the many deities they worship are ultimately aspects of Sanghyang Widi Wasa.

As Hinduism was adopted in Bali, some Indian gods were omitted while other specifically Balinese deities such as the rice goddess Dewi Sri or Rangda herself were adopted into the pantheon. Rangda is nowhere to be found in the Hinduism of India, and yet she had been required to coexist with Hindu gods. Although she for the most part retains an individual identity as a deity, she has also come to be associated with Dewi Durga, consort of Siwa the Destroyer.

Those with prior knowledge of Hindu deities may find it strange that Rangda is seen by many in Bali as an aspect of Durga when Kali would seem to be much more similar in nature. For those not well acquainted with these goddesses, I will start with a short description of each as they generally appear in their native India.

Although she enters into many stories, Durga is best known for her role as Mahisasuramardini, the slayer of the demon Mahisa. An abbreviated account runs as follows. The buffalo demon Mahisa had been granted a boon by the gods that rendered him invincible to any male opponent. He used this to defeat all the gods and usurp their positions. The gods became so angry at their inability to prevent this that the fiery energies emitted in their frustration and rage assumed the form of a fierce and beautiful goddess. Each of the gods gave this goddess, Durga, a weapon, and she successfully slew Mahisa, aided both by her tremendous military prowess and by the distracting effect of her beauty.

This is not the only story in which Durga makes an appearance, but iconographically it also defines her so that she is often depicted as a beautiful, many-armed, warrior goddess brandishing the weapons of all the gods. Although created out of the collective energies of the gods, Durga as she appears in this story does not act submissively to any man and is not defined solely in a wifely capacity. She is neither subordinated by nor lends her *sakti* to a male deity; in fact, she actually takes power from the gods to perform her heroic deeds. In addition, as a warrior Durga takes on and excels at a traditionally male function and is not concerned with helping find a way by which the gods may defeat Mahisa on their own and thus enjoy the resulting glory. Such behavior is appropriate enough for a goddess, especially one whose epithets include "The Inaccessible" and "The Unconquerable One," but her fierce independence makes her an unlikely candidate for a "perfect wife" in the mold of Sita, the heroine of the *Ramayana*.

This is not to say that Durga performs no function as a wife. As a result of an origin story in which Durga arose from Parvati (Parwati) as a fierce aspect of that goddess, Durga has come to take on the role of Shiva's consort. This association has also brought Durga to be regarded as the mother of Ganesha, Karttikeye, Sarasvati, and Lakshmi, and she is often depicted in this way during Durga Puja celebrations. However, the countless depictions of Durga with no companion save her lion vehicle reveal her domestic side as peripheral. Even when the goddess is shown with her children round her she appears distant from them, concentrating instead on the battle with Mahisa. More often, Durga is unmarried, or at least pretends to be so if we consider the stories that name Shiva as her consort, and lures some love-struck demon into battle by saying that her family will only allow her to marry one capable of beating her in combat. The would-be suitor is always slain. There is little of Rangda readily apparent in the above description of Durga.

This is not the case when we turn to Kali. Often referred to as "Terrible Mother" or as Shyama, "the dark one," Kali appears in Indian art as an emaciated, inkycomplexioned woman. She wears a garland of severed heads as a necklace and her mouth is shown ringed with the blood of her victims and with her reddened tongue sticking out. The protruding tongue of Kali is a direct visual parallel with that of Rangda. Although she is treated in some Hindu texts as an independent goddess standing alone, Kali may be considered another aspect of Devi, the Great Goddess, who is also worshipped alone. In addition, she is often associated with Shiva. When she appears as his consort in art, she is invariably dominant. She may be seen in the cemetery, dancing on the body of Shiva, who lies as if asleep or dead at her feet. In legends, Kali's participation in a battle often causes her to lose control and go on a frenzy of killing, causing mass destruction that threatens to destroy the world. An architectural work of the sixth to eighth centuries called the *Mana-sura-silpa-sastra* even prescribes the location of temples dedicated to Kali as near cremation grounds and away from the homes of all but the very lowest caste.[20]

Kali's predilection for graveyards, along with the appalling appearance and violently destructive nature make her seem an ideal model for the similarly disposed Rangda. Kali is not unknown in Bali, as is evidenced by the existence of a category of *usasa*, medical handbooks to be used by a *balian*, called *Kalimosada*, "the medicine of the goddess Kali."[21] Yet Balinese people clearly identify Rangda with Dewi Durga. This notion comes not only from those individuals I spoke with in Bali, but is also documented in the writings of McPhee, Covarrubias, Hobart, Leeman, Ramseyer, and others. Since these writers were not spotlighting Rangda in their studies, they did not make any reference to the possible implications of such an association on Rangda's character. I will venture to do so here. Whereas one of Kali's main characteristics is her tendency to fall into a state where she is totally out of control, Durga is much more selective as a destructive force. Kali's wild dances threaten to destroy the world that in her capacity as a deity she is supposed to protect. Durga's most popular epithet, Mahisasuramardini, comes from the great service she rendered to all the gods through her slaying of the demon who threatened to undermine the order of the cosmos.

In aligning Rangda with Durga rather than with Kali, the implication for Rangda's character and role in Balinese mythology is that she is ultimately not an enemy to order. She may be destructive, but it is not wantonly so. She protects against any forces that may serve to disrupt balance and is herself part of the balance.

Chapter 3

Truly Evil or Not?: Philosophical and Ethical Dimensions of Rangda

It is difficult to reconcile the Rangda who protects balance with the Rangda that Lansing describes as "the personification of the evil powers in the universe."[1] Despite this apparent disjunction, there is surprisingly little in the bulk of the writing about Rangda that questions the premise that she represents evil. It was only when I began to interview people in Bali that I realized this was not a premise to be taken for granted. Continuing my efforts to gain some understanding of how different people perceived Rangda, I asked my subjects whether Rangda was always evil, or if she ever did things that were helpful to the community. In cases where the subject was sufficiently fluent in English to understand that "evil" in English is defined as "something morally wrong or bad" that would ideally be absent from the world,[2] I was invariably corrected. Rangda may be frightening, destructive, even bad, but was not necessarily "evil". In *Healing Performances of Bali*, Angela Hobart stresses that while the Balinese tend to be "wary of her dark energies," Rangda is a highly complex entity.[3] Her presence may not be desired, but it is inevitable, and thus something to be expected and accepted. For some, although her powers may be rooted in darkness, she may even be considered as a force of good.

Destructiveness Does Not Rule Out Usefulness

Balinese experts on religion and culture with whom I made contact during my time there were willing to discuss their perceptions of Rangda. Other informants were not so forthcoming. With the exception of Pak Agung and Rucina Ballinger, both of whom had no reluctance to discuss any aspect of my topic, this second group was much less straightforwardly inclined to talk of Rangda's influence outside the usually discussed realms of mythology and dance-drama.

Truly Evil or Not?: Philosophical and Ethical Dimensions of Rangda

Ibu Agung and Murni initially approached the topic with trepidation, but opened up considerably when encouraged by others present, the husband in the first case, and, in the second, Joanna Moon, a British artist with whom both the subject and I were friendly. Three young women working at the Bali3000 Internet Café said that they did not know much about Rangda and that I should consult an expert such as a *balian*, who would be able to tell me about her. Although willing to chat with me in general, they could not be coaxed into offering any opinions on this subject, however humble. Such behavior may also come as a result of a fear that bad luck may come to the person who speaks of Rangda or of witchcraft in general, as Wikan found over the course of her research in North Bali during the 1980s. Magic could be dangerous to speak of, she discovered, as "the air itself may have ears, and the magicians themselves may be enraged at the talking."[4]

According to the *balian* I did interview, *rang* means "bad" or "something bad" and *da* means "don't." The name Rangda then translates as "Don't do bad," with the implication that this figure does not advocate wrongdoing. The manner in which my assistant Wayan translated this for me made it clear that he personally did not agree with that interpretation of the derivation of Rangda's name. Wayan had less trouble with the *balian*'s assertion that Rangda could not only attack people, but also protect them, thus performing a positive function for the community.

For Ibu Agung, Rangda is "sometimes bad, sometimes nice." She went on to remind me of the Bali Hindu concept that all deities are ultimately one, Sanghyang Widi Wasa, and that, therefore, Dewi Rangda has many names, from Dewi Durga to Dewi Sri to Dewi Parwati. All are one woman but all are also ultimately genderless. If an individual has in mind that the Rangda who spreads illness and fear is the same as the Dewi Sri who watches over the rice crop like a loving mother, that person is unlikely to perceive the Supreme Witch as one-dimensionally bad.

Arthana, the *pedanda* I spoke with, had this to say:

> Rangda does not always have a bad character. The bad character, that is just with the story [of Durga's unfaithfulness and also of Mahendradatta]. . . . In Bali, Rangda is always good. Only in the story is she a symbol of the bad character. It depends on the people who pray to [Rangda]. For example, the people who want good things, they will be blessed with good things.

Pak Agung felt that neither Rangda nor the black magic power she rules over are inherently bad. He looks at black magic as a sort of science that, if used appropriately and not to harm others, can, in fact, aid an individual to make contact with god. Black magic itself is not bad, only individual people who use and abuse the magic, guiding it by their emotions rather than their intellect: "Rangda is not always bad. She is very bad if someone disturbs her, [but] I think everyone is like that." Agung Rai's view of Rangda was similarly based on a policy of respect for (rather than simply fear of) her power. "The Queen of Evil," he said, "can be very wise."

These statements represent the views of merely a handful of individuals at a specific point in time. I do not present them as evidence that all Balinese feel that Rangda is primarily good, but merely as evidence that not everyone in Bali necessarily thinks of her as exclusively bad in the way that much of the literature on the subject would lead one to believe.

In her 1949 study of Rangda and Barong, Jane Belo described the witch as an entity that "looms out of the past, enormous, threatening, trailing all sorts of inglorious clouds, an evil nature and an evil reputation."[5] In that she is most typically depicted via the more traditional art forms such as carved masks and stone sculptures, and to the extent that these depictions follow long established iconographic conventions, Rangda does, indeed, seem to come at us from out of the past. This passage does, however, present us with a somewhat monolithic figure of the Queen of the Witches, who is unchanging in the perceptions she elicits from people in Bali fifty or sixty years after Belo's book was published.

In her capacity as Queen of the Witches, Rangda's role is not only to give power to Bali's *leyak* but also to keep them in check lest they spread too much evil and thus upset balance. True enough, in the Calonarang dance, Rangda comes to fight the forces of good in the form of the Barong, but she also comes with a more benevolent purpose. If the local *leyak* have become troublesome in the village, Rangda will call out a challenge for them to come and fight her. This is one of the reasons, according to the owners of my homestay in Ubud, that it can be so dangerous to dance Rangda.

Through the conduit of the masked dancer, Rangda calls out to all the *leyak* in the surrounding area: "*Leyaaaak!* Hey, all you *leyak*, come fight with me!" These lower-level witches, unable to control their anger at such taunting, come to the temple courtyard where the dance is being held and hurl volleys of black magic at Rangda via the human form she has possessed. This poses an obvious threat to the dancer, who can face sickness or even death at the hands of these *leyak*, but if the proper purification rites have been undertaken beforehand, the power of Rangda will protect this temporary vessel from harm. Rangda is not considered to be endangering the dancer for her own amusement or gratification but as a necessary means of keeping local *leyak* troubles under control.

Pak Agung told me that the result of the magical battle with Rangda often meant death for the lesser witch. At the very least the identity of the *leyak*, often previously only in the realm of suspicion, would be conclusively revealed to the other members of the community, who could then guard themselves against future attacks of black magic: "Sometimes Rangda will stop the spread of magic in the village. If we make an offering in the Pura Dalem, in the Temple of the Dead and center of magic, Rangda will stop the spread of magic everywhere in the village. So the Rangda does good."

Rangda also appears as a protective spirit in the form of the goddess Durga in some magical texts such as those dealt with by Hooykaas in *Drawings of Balinese Sorcery*. The extent to which an individual drawing of Durga is specifically intended to invoke the aspect of her that people in Bali would clearly recognize as Rangda is difficult to ascertain. However, since Rangda is associated with Durga and sometimes seen as synonymous with her, it is not unreasonable to identify Rangda's magical power with that possessed by Durga. In one drawing, she is called Dewi Dedewang, a name referring to her ability to frighten away all manner of supernatural beings. In another, she is given the title Durga Demba and endowed with the power to reverse the effects of encounters with vampires and other mishaps. This does not negate her identity as a malevolent being, as can be seen in other drawings intended to inspire fear and cause submission of the enemies of the individual for whom the images were made. Rangda/Durga has the ability to perform both malevolent and benevolent acts.

Rangda: An Element in Cosmic Balance

Despite initial appearances, Rangda is not an enemy to the state of order. First of all, Rangda's destructiveness need not be a bad thing, as she is not only the destroyer of order, but of the forces of chaos as well. This may seem an odd statement, given that I spoke of Rangda earlier on as a symbol of the forces of chaos (recall her identities as an angry spreader of illness and adversary of the Barong), but if we view her various roles as a "both and" rather than "either or" situation, there may be less of a feeling of contradiction. The fact that the Balinese are said to associate Rangda with Durga and not with Kali suggests that they see her destructiveness as something that is ultimately helpful to the maintenance of order and not as a tool for wanton devastation. Indeed, the individuals I spoke with were eager to impress on me that Rangda is a necessary part of "the balance."

Balance in the world is maintained, wrote anthropologist Unni Wikan, when "good and bad powers hold each other neutralized."[6] Unlike the People of the

Book (Jews, Christians, and Muslims) who see negative forces as contrary to order, Bali Hindus value these forces as an integral part of the whole. Christian art from Northern Europe is particularly rich in depictions of the demonic as an enemy to the desired and correct order of things. For example, a Hieronymus Bosch painting entitled *Death and the Miser* (*circa* 1490; National Gallery of Art, Washington, DC) centers around an avaricious old man on the edge of death whose accumulation of material possessions has fallen prey to Satan's minions. Startled by the figure of Death coming in through the door, the miser does not notice the demon who steals a bag of money out of his very hands and is equally oblivious to the angel at his shoulder who tries to show him the light of God. In pointing out the fact that a love of earthly riches does not bring one closer to God but instead attracts Satan, *Death and the Miser* acts as a warning against the deadly sin of greed. The work also implies that conversely, if the old man had not sinned by his miserliness, no demons would be present. Christianity carries with it an idea that evil is propagated through vice and eradicated through virtue.

This treatment of the subject of death and the demonic is in notable contrast with a 1936 work by Balinese artist Ida Bagus Putu Blatjok entitled *Cremation Preparations Observed by Sorcerers* (Fig. 6). This ink drawing shows a pavilion with a tiled roof that houses a body awaiting cremation. The carved wooden *lembu* (bull) sarcophagus in which the remains of high caste men were traditionally cremated stands ready in the center foreground, while villagers make themselves busy with the final preparations. These villages are unaware of the presence of the *leyak* in their midst and are equally unaware of the presence of the Barong in the top right-hand corner, as it is not a mask here but the invisible spirit of the actual being.

Where the Bosch panel depicts Satan's servants running amok despite the presence of one of God's angels, Blatjok's work shows *leyak* (who must answer to Rangda) rampaging through a village despite the presence of the powers of good in the form of the Barong. The relationship between the powers of good and evil, however, is quite different. In a Christian context, as in the Bosch painting, the desirable state of affairs would be the triumph of good over evil. This would be accomplished by the dying man's repentance, which would banish the Devil's servants. In the Bali Hindu context, it would be just as bad for the forces of light to get the upper hand as it would be for the forces of darkness to do so. Balance is the natural state of things, and the state to which things always and inevitably return. The occurrence of a disproportionate number of good things is a cause for concern for people in Bali who "believe it will be followed by something bad so there will be balance."[7] Blatjok's work is therefore without the implication that the Barong

Truly Evil or Not?: Philosophical and Ethical Dimensions of Rangda

Figure 6. *Cremation preparations observed by sorcerers* by Ida Bagus Putu Blatjok (1936). Originally published in Hildred Geertz, *Images of Power: Balinese Paintings Made for Gregory Bateson and Margaret Mead* (Honolulu: University of Hawaii Press, 1994). Courtesy of Hildred Geertz and the Bateson-Mead collection

should ideally triumph over Rangda's followers, for this could only be a temporary victory for the forces of light that on another occasion would surely be offset by a victory for darkness. The Barong in the painting watches over the village and will prevent the *leyak* from getting out of hand and causing imbalance, but the forces of darkness have just as much place in that world as do those of light.

The idea of Rangda's more benevolent role in the Calonarang dance in no way negates or even lessens her symbolic importance as an opposing force to the Barong. Rangda symbolizes black magic and the forces of darkness, while Barong is for white magic and the forces of light. Together, they symbolize balance. Even when Rangda is fighting Barong, she is viewed as a necessary part of balance, without whom harmony and order in the universe would be impossible. As an expression of this, when not in use, the Rangda mask is not housed in the Pura Dalem as one might expect given her connection with that temple. Instead, she resides in the Pura Desa, the village temple, together with the mask of the Barong. "While they are together," said the *pemangku* I interviewed, "they are the symbol of life, because in Bali, good and evil, day and night, we can't avoid that in this life. It is a balance that makes life. There is bad, there is good. They are always together."

Potent enough when taken individually, Rangda and Barong as a pair have tremendous power that can be used for the benefit of the community. I was able to witness this during an annual ceremony at Pura Luhur on the slopes of Gunung Batakau that Wayan took me to. Here Barongs and Rangdas from all over the Gianyar regency were assembled (Figs. 7-8). After holy water was distributed by the priests in attendance and offerings were made by the people from the surrounding area, all the Barongs and Rangdas were led in a procession through a number of surrounding villages. Wayan informed me that the purpose of the ritual was one of purification and would help to prevent outbreaks of illness in the area.

Encouraging Humans to Adhere to Bali Hindu Traditions

Another way in which Rangda helps maintain order in the long run rather than working to destroy it is through disturbing those who have failed to make proper offerings to the gods. This aspect of her behavior was not explicitly mentioned in any of the anthropological literature I found on Bali, but it came up a number of times in interviews. It is necessary, as mentioned earlier, for Balinese people to regularly attend to the needs of the unseen beings with whom they share this world. This takes the form of *dewa yadnya*, rituals performed as worship of the gods, and *buta yadnya*, rituals that pacify demons and other malevolent spirits. These range

Truly Evil or Not?: Philosophical and Ethical Dimensions of Rangda

Figure 7. Barong procession at Pura Luhur

Figure 8. Rangda procession at Pura Luhur

from small scale daily rituals to annual regency-wide ceremonies to the island-wide ceremony *Eka Dasa Rudra*, held once a century and intended to purify not only the island but also the whole universe. All are seen as important. If an individual or community becomes somewhat lax in these duties, the gods become annoyed at the lack of attention being paid to them and Rangda is invited to cause trouble for the guilty parties.

People who have recently suffered a series of misfortunes will often discover through the visions of a *balian* that they have failed to make the proper offerings and are thus feeling the anger of the gods at the hands of Rangda. When I asked the *balian* I interviewed whether Rangda was always bad or if she ever did things that are helpful to the people or to the gods, he said it all depends upon the individual people themselves: "Rangda can attack the people, but she can also protect the people. When we do something wrong, I mean contrary to religious teachings, Rangda attacks. And then when we do something good, Rangda will protect us." The *pemangku* with whom I had spoken a few weeks earlier made a similar statement when asked about Rangda's influence upon people in their everyday lives: "Rangda disturbs people who don't care for the gods, especially Hindus who don't make offerings every day." He went on to explain that it is Rangda's job to control people: "Rangda kind of controls the people who are praying to the gods. Rangda has rules that control the people, Balinese people, in their prayers to the gods." Since Rangda will only disturb those who have in some way contravened the rules of the Bali Hindu religion, she can be said to encourage people to stay on the correct path. In this way, her destructive force also helps to maintain the order of the Bali Hinduism.

As can be seen from the last example and from the *balian*'s interpretation of the word "Rangda" as an instruction to the people to avoid doing bad things, there is a strongly didactic element in Rangda. Those who do not pay sufficient respect to the myriad unseen forces as set out by Bali Hindu traditions are threatened with a visitation from Rangda. People in Bali likely learn as I did, from priests and elders, that she will attack those who behave contrary to the lessons of the religion.

If by invoking the name and image of Rangda, priests are indeed successful in deterring members of the community from straying from religion as they have defined it, then those people benefit greatly from the way in which Rangda is constructed. If one were to ask "Who does the figure of Rangda empower in this context?," the answer would likely be those who seek to perpetuate a central role for religion in Balinese society and their own roles as guardians of this knowledge.

As the way in which Rangda is constructed varies according to context, so do the groups who benefit. For example, the social function performed by Rangda as a means of preserving modes of worship can be quite different from the one she performs with regards to the proper place of women in Bali, an issue to which I will now turn.

Chapter 4

Implications of Rangda for Constructing the Feminine

Thus far I have largely glossed over the possible age and gender implications inherent in a figure such as Rangda. While the discussion of Rangda and gender is well worth a study in its own right, there remains so much that is uncertain about the full implications for the figure of Rangda to the construction of gender as it is envisioned in Bali that this discussion presents only an entry point to the material in the hope that others will go on to give it the attention it deserves. To Euro-North Americans, especially those have been brought up with Western feminism, the way Rangda is constructed can be a cause for concern. By "Western feminism," I refer to the type of feminism encapsulated by the following excerpt from an essay by Margot Mifflin: "The failure of the women's movement in the late '60's was its almost exclusively white middle- and upper-class orientation. It basically remains that way, but the difference is that white women are inviting women of color to participate, and unless women of color join them in their endeavor, no amount of change can take place."[1]

According to Margo Machida in her essay "(re)-Orienting", this feminism has been criticized by Asian women:

> [Asian women feel that] the traditional Western feminist movement, originating in white middle-class concerns, is frequently seen as insisting that the behavior and needs of women from other cultures and ethnic backgrounds be evaluated by their standards. ... Asian women often consider feminists' critiques of patriarchy and emphasis on individual independence as a threat to family unity.[2]

These statements underline the fact that the feminism(s) designed for and by Euro-North American women within specific parameters of race and class does not address issues specific to women outside these guidelines. To a Euro-North American woman, the fact that the face of evil in Bali is an old, widowed woman may appear to vilify mature, independent women. Rucina Ballinger, who had been living in Bali for over fifteen years at the time of our interview told me that one of the things she found most disturbing about Rangda is that "the Balinese use an older woman, unattached to a man, as something frightening." When I interviewed Murni, a woman who had divorced her Balinese husband when he wanted to take a second wife who could give him a child, and then Ibu Agung, who co-ran a homestay with her husband, neither expressed a similar concern when speaking about their perceptions of Rangda. One could attribute this to the subjects' self-censorship after having internalized the patriarchal values of their culture, or one could question whether a negative view of Rangda as an independent being can specifically target women in a culture where all, male or female, are said to place a high value on family ties and dislike being alone. Until a study of Rangda is undertaken by Balinese feminist, it will be difficult to know what interpretation best fits the realities of the women on Bali.

Does Rangda Vilify Women?

What is there in the way that Rangda is constructed that might lead one to think that she vilifies old women or even women generally? For a start, if we assemble a number of the dualities so important to Balinese cosmology—life and death, good and evil, white magic and black magic, *kaja* (toward the mountain, realm of the gods) and *kelod* (toward the sea, realm of the demons), male and female, right and left, day and night, Barong and Rangda—we find Rangda placed firmly on the left hand side of the equation. In fact, women in general are placed in this half of the duality, where "female" exists alongside death, evil, black magic, *kelod*, left, and night. If read in the "either/or" rather than in the "both/and" sense, this system of organization seems to suggest that the feminine is associated with the negative in Balinese thought. Rangda, as described in the documentary film *Bali: Mask of Rangda*, is "the witch, the widow-mother who devours her own children, who robs souls from the graveyard and feasts on human entrails, who brings pestilence and famine, she is the left-hand path, the supreme sorceress of black magic."[3] The fact that the ruler over negative forces is a female underscores the connection between those forces and the feminine.

In her book *Images of Power: Balinese Paintings Made for Gregory Bateson and Margaret Mead*, Hildred Geertz attempts to downplay the implications of Rangda for the construction of the feminine. In her discussion of Ida Bagus Nyoman Tjeta's *Balinese "Witches,"* she consciously uses the term *rangda* as a translation of "sorcerer or deity in ferocious form" to reflect the fact that men as well as women practice black magic. Yet all the figures in the painting are clearly given female form, and when Geertz speaks more at length of sorcery, she uses the work *leyak* with a feminine pronoun. Geertz summarizes the appearance of the generic *rangda*, but states firmly that "femininity is not central to the idea, since a male sorcerer on a violent rampage may take the shape of a rangda."[4] In a sense, femininity is indeed not the central issue, in that not only females can become *leyak*. That said, Unni Wikan defines *leyak* specifically as "females of inborn evil, with the capacity to transform themselves into any shape."[5] Even if *leyak* powers can be found in men, the concept of male sorcerers taking on the female form in order to perform deeds of violence and destruction would appear to make a case for the association of the feminine with evil rather than against it. It is true that this is not the only form that a *leyak* may take, as they possess the ability to transform themselves into a variety of animals such as a pig, a monkey, or a goat, and the more powerful ones can change into simple white cloth (as opposed to that used by Rangda, which is decorated with black magic mantras) or a small tower. The highest form of transformation, however, is into the semblance of Rangda herself.

Despite the fact that *leyak* tend to favor the guise of animals or women while pursuing their destructive impulses, it would be unfair to say that this represents a dim view taken by Balinese culture of women in general. The existence of the beloved rice goddess Dewi Sri is a case in point. One could safely say that Dewi Sri is the antithesis of Rangda—young, beautiful, gentle, and benevolent. Also a goddess of beauty, Dewi Sri is often found in the form of a *cili* (also spelled *tjili*), a stylized silhouette of a slender young woman wearing a large headdress of flowers made out of various plant materials. Dewi Sri is sometimes spoken of as the Rice Mother, and when the time comes that Bali's human inhabitants must harvest her children, it is customary to use a small blade that can be concealed in one's hand to cut the rice. This is done out of respect for the goddess, so that she may not be frightened or offended by the act's necessary violence. Given the positive attitude that one sees toward this goddess, it would be incorrect to characterize the construction of Rangda as a straightforward reflection of a general Balinese attitude toward women. Could the same be said for old women though? Is Rangda perhaps a reflection of an attitude that is not so much sexist as ageist?

Implications for the Treatment of Widows and Older Women

Based on the research done by Wikan for *Managing Turbulent Hearts* and backed up by my own research, there is little or no evidence for a Balinese viewpoint in which all women are in some way associated with Rangda. When the discussion turns to elderly widows, however, one gets more of a sense that a mental connection is made, albeit small, between these widows and the widow who is the Queen of Black Magic.

As well as being an analysis of the famous "Balinese poise," Wikan's book is also a story of a few young women with whom she spent a good deal of her time in Bali. In one anecdote she tells of going with her friend Issa to the home of a high ranking widow who was well known for her refined nature and religious piety. During the visit, both hostess and guests behaved impeccably in accordance with Balinese social graces, but some time afterward Issa revealed to her friend that she had, in fact, been terrified of the woman. She was concerned that the hostess, for some unknown reason, did not like her. Perhaps she had at some time in the past unwittingly caused offense, and now the woman sought to do her harm through black magic.[6]

What could possibly lead Issa to suspect her gracious hostess, a woman who by all appearances was full of kindness? Could it be because she was a widow? In a society in which sex roles give lower status to women who are not wives or mothers and in which widows are often linked with *leyak*, it is quite probable that this woman's marital status would place her under suspicion. Wikan did not state in her anecdote whether or not this widow had any children, and it is difficult to say what impact this information could have had on the level of suspicion directed at her. While sometimes a widow with children is treated with considerable respect in honor of her status as a mother, Rangda herself had a daughter and has been called the Queen of Evil all the same.

In another anecdote, this time revolving around a young woman named Suriati, Wikan writes of the necessity felt by her friend to keep her true feelings under wraps. Suriati had just suffered a great personal tragedy with the sudden death of her fiancé, but it was vital that she present herself to the world as gracious and calm, not sad and bitter: "I do not want them to think or say that I have a broken heart, for then they will mock me. Then they will say, 'Oh, you're a widow!' and they will laugh. It is very bad if you are sad and they laugh. That is why we keep our sadness."[7]

From this statement, it is quite clear that it is undesirable to be compared to a widow. When I asked Wayan to clarify his use of the word "widow," he led me to believe that the term served to denote both women who were single because their husbands had died and women who had never married. Wikan's anecdote about the young woman, betrothed but not yet married, who feared that people would call her a widow if she showed grief at the loss of her intended also supports the idea that one need not have been married to be seen as a widow.

Implications for the Treatment of Widows and Older Women

In my interviews, practitioners of black magic were mentioned twice. In both cases they were identified as mature single females. According to one of the people with whom I spoke, this was purely coincidental; according to the other, it was indicative of a cultural bias against independent women. Pak Agung spoke briefly of an old woman in his village of whom most people were extremely frightened: "Most people don't want to touch [her]," he told me. I asked him if this was because she was a widow, and he said "because she is a widow, and also because she has strong black magic power." However, when I went on to ask whether this meant that widows were more likely to practice black magic or that people in Bali were more frightened of widows than of other people, he thought not. When the question was put to him in this way, he disagreed with the notion that the Balinese would more likely be suspicious of a widowed woman.

Rucina Ballinger also knew of a woman who was thought to be a witch. In this case, the woman in question, her husband's maternal aunt, was technically not a widow, in the English language sense of the word, but a spinster, having remained unmarried rather than having lost her husband. When Ms Ballinger married into the household of which this woman was a part, she was advised not to eat any food prepared by her, as it may have been infused with black magic spells. Despite the fact that after many years of close contact she never saw her aunt perform any of the acts usually associated with witchcraft—nightflights, meditation in the graveyard or Pura Dalem, nocturnal rituals—the woman was generally believed to be a witch.

For someone raised outside of this culture, this allegation had absolutely no supporting evidence. If this old, unmarried aunt was not considered a witch because of any suspicious actions, then why did members of the family and the community at large feel so certain that she practiced black magic? Ms Ballinger felt the answer to be at the same time simple and disturbing: "I think that all over the world, men, and to a certain extent women, are very threatened by women who don't have to be married to validate themselves."

Older single women would thus be more of a threat than young single women, as with younger women there is still seen to be a potential for eventual marriage. Although the notion of the independent and happily single woman as a threat to the male ego comes from a Euro-North American feminist mode of thought, another way in which the stigma of the unmarried woman could be viewed is as a threat not to individual men, but to the male/female balance that underlies all aspects of traditional Balinese society. Kaja McGowan addressed this in her essay "Balancing on Bamboo: Women in Balinese Art": "Central to the configuration of male and female, usually the conjugal couple as a single entity, is the importance placed in traditional Balinese society on bearing children, the woman's procreative capacities being connected symbolically with the renewal of the crops and the fecundity of the land."[8]

If traditional Balinese cosmology places great spiritual importance on procreation and the coupling of male and female as symbols of fertility of the land and the harmony of the gods, then women must be encouraged to fulfill their roles as wives and mothers or risk throwing off the balance of the whole.

In their essay "Sex Roles and the Sexual Division of Labor," Francine Rainone and Janice Moulton wrote that: "Where there are expectations and standards in a society, there will be rewards and penalties for not fitting some patterns or carrying out some functions."[9] If getting married and raising a family are expected roles for women, then those women who follow this pattern are rewarded with higher social status and those who do not are penalized with lower status. Ibu Agung felt that all people wanted to marry, if only to ensure that in a country without pension plans older people will have their children to look after them when they are no longer able to work. Her husband added that, according to Balinese religion, an unmarried or childless woman is not a perfect human being and will be punished in the afterlife.

Men are not immune to the pressures to marry and start a family. Ballinger observed in our interview that pressure appeared to mount for men after the age of thirty, with members of the community asking the same question Ibu Agung admitted to asking: "When will you be married?" A more concrete form of pressure comes from the fact that men are not allowed to become members of the village *banjar* (community administrative body) unless they are married. Even men who are known to be homosexual are expected eventually to marry and join the *banjar*. However, despite the fact that there is a degree of stigma attached to remaining unmarried for both sexes, there appears to be more at stake for women in that they do not inherit from their family. The land and house go to the sons, while daughters are expected to go and live with their husbands' families when they marry. A woman who chooses not to marry is thus placed at an extreme financial disadvantage.

Among the Balinese men and women I spoke with, the general consensus was that their society looked upon marriage as the natural state of things and that it would require much courage on the part of an individual who wished to remain single. "In Bali," the schoolteacher I interviewed in Tabanan told me, "people hear the word 'widow' and think of Rangda. It functions as a lesson for people, not to become a widow. That is why Balinese women try hard to avoid becoming widows."

That is why they have to marry." Rangda here acts as a negative example: she is an angry, destructive woman working alone, that is to say, without a man.

With Rangda, as with Balinese women who have the misfortune (by Balinese standards) to be likened to her, chronological age is less of a factor than independence. Women in general are not seen in the same negative light as Rangda. Arthana, the *pedanda* I spoke with, maintained that "when women are more respected than men, there will be peace forever. In some ways, women are more respected than men, because a woman has a great ability. She is the one who has children and takes care of the family."

Nor are all old women looked down upon or feared, as related by Ms Ballinger with regards to her Balinese mother-in-law. This woman was a widow and the oldest person in the family compound, and yet it was she who was consulted about the undertaking of particular rituals and ceremonies. Why should her words carry weight when those of the unmarried aunt in the same compound did not? According to Ballinger, it was because her mother-in-law had been married and had had children. This makes sense when one looks at the *pedanda*'s concept of the ideal woman as wife and mother. Marriage and the raising of a family appear to be all-important in the Balinese conception of a woman's social role.

With regards to Rangda, the fact that she was not only a mother but also motivated by a desire to marry off her daughter seems to be strangely overlooked when she is spoken of as a negative force. Perhaps it is thought that she was not a good mother because it her practice of black magic prevented her daughter from finding a suitor in the first place and because she sought a violent solution to the problem. Whether the issue of her motherhood is included or viewed as an exception, Rangda could still overall be said to be a summation of everything that a Balinese woman should not be. In this way, she helps to define what is thought to be proper and improper behavior for a woman in that culture.

Rangda: Negative Example of Appropriate Feminine Behavior

When I say that Rangda helps to define feminine behavior protocols in Bali, this does not mean that she is the causal factor in this relationship. I would argue that she is more symptomatic in the sense that she is constructed in accordance with existing sensibilities. She is an amplification of them. In order to give a sense of how this works, it is necessary to attempt a sketch of what actions and character traits constitute proper versus improper behavior for a woman living in Balinese society. Wikan's research, based as it is on her close personal contact with a number of Balinese women over a period of time, is quite helpful here.

To begin with, the title of Wikan's book, *Managing Turbulent Hearts*, comes from the emphasis she witnessed among the Balinese on not giving way to one's emotions, and instead maintaining at all times a "clear, bright face." Rangda-like displays of anger cause bad feelings, and there is a sense that people who dwell on their own problems rather than seeking to maintain harmony in the community are viewed as selfish: "If someone sits there brooding, people will say he is thinking about himself only, not the whole of our people."[10]

Wikan used the story of Suriati as a case in point. Despite suffering the effects of a great personal tragedy in the form of the sudden death of a loved one, it was vital for the young woman to repress her feelings of sorrow and loss and to carry herself in a calm, even cheerful, way. Not to do so would be socially disastrous, and her punishment would be ridicule, an ever-effective means of humiliating deviants in any society into adhering to social convention.

I do not wish to suggest, and I doubt that Wikan does, that this behavior is limited to Bali's *women*. I would argue, however, that men alone are provided with a venue for expressing their "turbulent hearts." This occurs in the battle between Barong and Rangda where some of the dancers go into trance and attack first the witch and then themselves. The violence of this rite in which members of a community who normally coexist peacefully will often turn their blades on each other functions as a cathartic experience.

The documentary film *Bali: Mask of Rangda* states that "in sacred drama, in full public view, they are acting out the hatred and violence that can tear apart the individual mind or social fabric and they are exorcising it." By acting out the anger that the Balinese acknowledge lurks in all of us in a controlled setting, the dancers are able to prevent these forces from taking over in everyday life. However, only males are found doing this. At one time *kris* dancers, as the trance dancers who carry traditional daggers are called, could be male or female, but this practice appears to have stopped at some point after the 1950s. In contemporary times, women have no such form of release, and to them is left the task of maintaining that "clear, bright face" at all times, in life as in the female-danced roles in the dance-drama.

In this context, Rangda is a clear example of how not to act. In the story of Randeng Dirah, the widow's response to the shunning of her daughter by the community's eligible bachelors is one of intense anger. Rather than managing her feelings and projecting an image of calm and cheerfulness, she uses magic motivated by rage to spread an epidemic. As Wikan writes, "sadness and anger are anathema to health and happiness,"[11] and should therefore be avoided for the sake of oneself and the community. Bad feelings toward another person will often turn into what the Balinese call "anger sickness," for which the natural progression is thought to be gratification through black magic.

Rangda's violent behavior throughout the Randeng Dirah story is the perfect example of this principle in action. According to the Balinese behavioral code, she ought to have responded to the offense against her daughter with cheerfulness, acting as if it did not matter in the least. Her ability to maintain impeccable manners despite the way in which her daughter had been ill treated would lead the guilty parties to compare their behavior to hers and to find themselves lacking, and thus shame them into doing right by the girl.

Rangda can also function as a negative example of feminine behavior in her incarnation as Durga. When asked about the relationship between Rangda and Durga, I Ketut Arthana, the *pedanda* I interviewed, told the following story. Siwa asked his wife Durga to go into the woods, ostensibly to look for a particular food item, but, in fact, because he wished to test her loyalty to him. After his wife departed, Siwa changed his outward appearance into that of a cattle-herder and followed her into the woods. Durga met the cattle-herder, not knowing it was her husband, and found herself attracted to him. The two made love, after which Durga returned to Heaven where Siwa was waiting for her. He asked her what had happened in the woods. She lied, saying nothing at all had transpired, an act that sent Siwa into a fury with the knowledge that not only was his wife unfaithful to him but that she had also lied about it. Durga then became Rangda, a symbol of bad character.

After relating this legend, Arthana was anxious to make it clear that the idea of Rangda as a symbol of bad character is limited to this story. His point was that although Rangda's character may be simplified for the purposes of didactic tales meant to discourage behavior that runs contrary to the culture's social mores, it is still understood that the real Rangda is not so one-dimensional. Nonetheless, she is used here, as elsewhere, to demonstrate how a Balinese woman should and should not behave.

Returning to the question posed earlier with regards to the conventions of worship, we may again ask "Who does the figure of Rangda empower in this context?," the context here being the construction of gender roles. When Rangda is held up to a woman as a negative example, that woman may feel that she is not meant to define herself independently from her husband and children and that she must face the role divinely given to her uncomplainingly and with a "clear, bright face." Rangda is not the sole emblem of such modes of thought, but works in tandem with other aspects of Balinese mythology, such as images of hell described by Kaja McGowan in which women who remained childless in life are punished after death by being made to suckle giant caterpillars.[12]

Elements such as these function together to present an image in which a Balinese woman who wishes to avoid being like Rangda or suffering after death is married with children and goes about smilingly performing the ritual tasks allotted to the household's female members. It is doubtful that women in Bali would feel empowered by a mythology with such clearly defined and narrow parameters for fulfillment. I would suggest that the men in this society who benefit the most. Ibu Agung referred to the practical side of having children, in that they would be able to look after her when she grew old, but it was the men I interviewed who looked upon childbirth as more of a higher calling for women. If it was truly the feeling of all Balinese women that being an ideal wife and mother was the pinnacle of womanly existence, it seems unlikely that there would be a need for either the negative example of Rangda or the threat of divine punishment for those who failed to comply.

Rawana and Siwa: Male Equivalents to Rangda

Much of the feminist objection to Rangda stems from the fact that the face of evil in Bali is a feminine one. Are women there really viewed as more closely linked to the negative element than men? According to the examples presented above, this may well be the case for some groups of Balinese women, namely those operating outside the prescribed social activities. It would not be true to say, however, that women are singled out exclusively because of the existence of a *Queen* of Evil. *Bali: Mask of Rangda* presents the demon king Rawana as a male equivalent to Rangda. Rawana is the villain of the *Ramayana*, the epic story of the Hindu tradition. Motivated by lust for King Rama's wife Sita, Rawana kidnaps her with the help of his great magical powers. In mask form, Rawana's iconography follows a similar pattern to Rangda's: he has bulging eyes and large, flared nostrils. His pointed teeth, although not as pronounced as those of the witch, are set in thick, red lips with an overbite, suggestive of his violent temper and greedy nature. To compare a person with Rawana is said to be seen as a great insult in Indonesia.[13]

In a series of magical drawings published by C. Hooykaas in *Drawings of Balinese Sorcery*, there appears a figure labeled "Ki Chalon Arang." For Hooykaas, this drawing, included in a section devoted to spells causing death and decay, is "obviously a male derivative of the witch Chalon Arang."[14] As this is the only information he provides, it is difficult to know how commonly the image may occur in magical drawings. However, the existence of even one such drawing suggests that envisioning the powers of death and destruction in masculine rather than feminine form is not a totally alien concept in Bali. Indeed, the god Siwa is the embodiment of these forces and is himself seen as the Lord of the Pura Dalem.

The existence of a character such as Rawana or of a male equivalent to the witch from the Calonarang alters the extent to which women can be said to be vilified in Balinese mythology. Rangda is not the only wicked sorcerer in Bali, so the practice of harmful black magic and the inability to control one's emotions is not likely to be associated exclusively with women. Both Rawana and Rangda could be said to function as negative examples of behavior for the two sexes, respectively. Through their violent outbursts of anger, lust, or jealousy, they demonstrate to Balinese men and women how not to conduct themselves. The threat of being compared by one's peers to either character underscores the lesson.

This said, I still do not want to draw out the comparison too far. Two factors stand in the way of interpreting Rangda and Rawana as totally equivalent. First, there is the matter of context. The *Ramayana* is presented as a ceremonial offering to the gods and for the enjoyment of spectators. It is not seen as magically powerful and is therefore safely performed in the mid-space of a temple. The Calonarang is a sacred exorcism rite held outside the temple proper and close to the crossroads and graveyard, both ritually dangerous places where darker forces may be met with on their home ground. Also, Rawana is killed at the end of the *Ramayana*. He does not represent the principle of darkness, but is but one example of its occurrence. There is more a sense that Rawana is simply the villain in the play, whereas Rangda's spirit comes down through her mask to battle the Barong and challenge the local *leyak*.

The second factor was brought to my attention over the course of my interview with the *pemangku*. Through my interpreter, I asked him if there existed in Balinese mythology a male equivalent to Rangda. Despite countless rephrasings in the most straightforward language possible, this turned out to be the only question I asked during my stay in Bali that neither interpreter nor subject understood. That this should go unanswered while other, to my mind, more complex topics were discussed with relative ease, suggests to me that none of the Balinese present during the interview consciously held Rawana as an obvious male equivalent to Rangda. If it is through her association with the similarly disposed Rawana that we decide Rangda does not serve to vilify women, is the hypothesis still valid if many Balinese do not hold such an association?

Rawana is not the only male figure with whom Rangda may be linked. One of the epithets for the god Siwa, both in India and on Bali, is "The Destroyer." Durga, as she occurs in India, also bears this epithet. Theirs is a focused destruction, ultimately combating the forces of chaos. They exist in a context where death and destruction are seen as a necessary part of the cycle of life and death and function to allow these to happen with a minimum of chaos. In Bali, Durga (as Rangda) is sometimes a symbol of focused destruction and sometimes of a seemingly more chaotic destruction, such as the spreading of epidemics. She is still seen as a necessary part of the cycle of existence.

Bali Hinduism, as was said above, especially reveres the god Siwa. He might be called "The Destroyer," but since life and death occur as part of a never-ending cycle, in being a power of Death he is also seen as the creator of new life. Durga, and therefore Rangda as an aspect of Durga, may be seen either as Siwa's consort or as one of his feminine manifestations, since all deities are ultimately one. Interviewees who mentioned Siwa tended to speak of him as the goddess's husband. Despite the fact that death temples are dedicated to both deities, none of my contacts suggested Siwa as a male equivalent to Rangda when this question was posed. It seems to be that Rangda's designation as the Queen of Evil is not generally carried over to apply to the god of destruction as the "King of Evil."

Barong and Rangda as Aspects of Siwa and his Consort

Bali: Mask of Rangda brings up another point with regards to Rangda, gender, and her relationship to Siwa. In the film, the struggle between Barong and Rangda is highlighted in regards to its social value as a reenactment of the on-going struggle between the forces of good and evil. In addition, the film makes a passing reference to Barong as an incarnation of Siwa. It is interesting to note that there is little mention of this interpretation elsewhere in the literature on Bali, although Covarrubias did write that Barong is known by many titles.[15]

If Barong is an aspect of Siwa as Rangda is an aspect of Durga, then they could be viewed as consorts as well as combatants. In Hindu mythology, both Siwa and Durga take "The Destroyer" as one of their titles. It seems quite appropriate then that the demonic forms of Barong and Rangda should represent the male and female elements of the destructive principle. It should be remembered, however, that in the context of the Barong dance, Barong is seen as a benevolent force dedicated to maintaining order. Barong does not initiate violent acts, but only acts to prevent the witch from doing so. Rangda, Durga's incarnation, is clearly the more destructive of the two, implying that of the two deities bearing the title "Destroyer," the goddess is the more destructive.

Envisioning Barong and Rangda as husband and wife adds another dimension to the way the two function as a pair. The idea that they are not only sparring partners but also spouses gives more meaning to their ability to become the symbol of balance when they are brought together. Balance is created when opposing forces are equal, but when those forces are seen as a couple in the truest, most literal sense, the Balinese concept that balance is the natural state of things is underlined: husband and wife work together in order to maintain harmony. This, in turn, reflects Balinese social organization in which all tasks are divided up into men's work and women's work, with the idea that people will form couples in which the husband does his part and the wife hers. This division of labor along gender lines is particularly apparent in the making of offerings, where women are responsible for creating daily offerings from vegetable materials, and men are responsible for those offerings needed at larger ceremonies that require the use of meat products. Francine Brinkgreve, author of "The Cili and Other Female Images in Bali," speaks of this division as a manifestation of the complimentary opposition between male and female, a part of the "socio-cosmic dualism" that has traditionally been an integral part of Balinese culture.[16] The balance symbolized by Barong/Siwa and Rangda/Durga thus carries over into the human realm where individual couples could be seen as representing this balance in microcosm.

Before proceeding further, it should be noted that not everyone in Bali necessarily views Rangda and Barong as Durga and Siwa, respectively. Lansing lists several variations he was told of by informants. According to one, Rangda is Iswara (another name for Siwa) and Barong is Brahma, while another said Durga was Rangda's mother. Another interpretation yet was that Rangda derives her power from Siwa and Barong from Banas Pati Raja, Lord of the Jungle. However, if one accepts as a possible interpretation the link between the following pairs—Barong/Rangda, Siwa/Durga, husband/wife—balance may not be the only implication of the association.

I have presented the husband-wife relationship of Barong and Rangda as evidence of the underlying harmony between the two, but what is to prevent one from looking at this equation the other way round? That is to say, could the depiction in performance art of a husband-wife relationship made up of the ever fighting Barong and Rangda be construed as evidence of conflict on some level between a man and woman who are married? Looked at in this light, the fight between the beast and the witch in sacred dance is a literal acting out of the battle of the sexes. In the performance filmed for *Bali: Mask of Rangda*, there is a segment of the dance in which the bulky Barong first envelopes and then pins down the comparatively smaller Rangda who, lacking in physical bulk to retaliate in force, bides her time and then lets fly a volley of shrieked curses. Could this conceivably be an archetypal depiction of domestic violence?

A more common interpretation has Rangda derived from Uma, the gentle aspect of Siwa's consort. As recounted by Angela Hobart in *Healing Performances of Bali*, the story goes that after Sanghyang Widi Wasa created the world he sent the divine couple to inspect it. Uma went first and Siwa after her, each in turn being overcome by the beauty of the earth and allowing their passions to take over. They became possessed and took on the demonic forms of Rangda and Barong, together causing chaos in the world. To save the world from this chaos, the other deities put on a shadow play telling the story of Kama and Ratih, themselves aspects of Siwa and Uma.[17] The couple was calmed, regained the ability to distance themselves from earthly desires, and returned to Heaven. A vision of the two as they had appeared in their terrible forms was given to the Balinese so that their dance could be performed as a reminder to humans of the dangers of giving free rein to one's feelings.

This origin story is particularly interesting in that it depicts both Rangda and Barong as divine beings with uncontrolled emotions. As Hobart writes, "The earth trembled to contain the fiery passions of Rangda and Barong Ket. They devoured many humans and suffering became intense."[18] *They* devoured. Barong's appealing, sometimes even described as puppy-like, behavior in performance and his role as a protector can make it possible to forget that he still comes from where the wild things are. He is Lord of the Forest as Rangda is Queen of the Witches. Perhaps the Barong of the dance has just been slightly more successful in reining in his emotions than has his counterpart. In that case, what he fights is not Rangda herself, only her excessive wildness.

The False Woman: Rangda Danced by a Man

Although the Rangda of myth is clearly a female being, indeed so much so that my attempt to question her gender was met with incredulity, the fact remains that the Rangda of the Calonarang dance is traditionally performed by a male. Each person I interviewed about this had a slightly different opinion as to why or the extent to which this may be the case. For example Agung Rai, director of ARMA, said that women were generally not encouraged to dance Rangda, but that in certain areas the dancer could be either male or female. He also stressed the danger of wearing

The False Woman: Rangda Danced by a Man

the Rangda mask and the need for the dancer to undergo purifying rituals. Unsaid but implied is the fact that the menstrual cycle renders women "ritually impure" for one week out of every month, during which time it would be highly dangerous, even sacrilegious, for a woman to perform a sacred dance. Murni said that women are not allowed to dance Rangda, mostly due to the issue of menstruation, but that they would not wish to anyway out of fear of the power of the mask and the spirits it would call forth. Pak and Ibu Agung felt that it the choice of a male dancer was due to more mundane physical matters: specifically, that a man can carry the often heavy mask with its mass of wild hair, and a man's voice has a volume and pitch more conducive to shouting challenges to the local *leyak*.

From the way it is dealt with in the books on Bali and from discussions I had with people there, it appears to be universally known in Bali that the human behind the mask of the witch is male. The idea of the "false woman" is readily apparent at a point in *Bali: Mask of Rangda* where the dancer is unmasked and proceeds to do a circuit of the temple courtyard clad in only a portion of his costume. Clothed in this manner, he becomes simply a man in women's clothing with fake breasts. Transvestitism and the use of costume to alter identity are not uncommon in many cultures, from tales of a Trickster figure in North American aboriginal art, to the Tibetan Uncle Tompa, to the men of Tomman Island in Vanuata who perform a dance stolen from the island's women. Rituals involving a masquerade as a member of the opposite sex have been described by writers such as Mircea Eliade and Wendy Doniger O'Flaherty as a simulation of androgyny and through this "the integration of opposites and the return to chaos."[19] Whether the ultimate state of existence is thought to belong to the realm of chaos or that of harmony depends upon the cosmology of the culture in question. I would argue that in the case of Bali, the integration of opposites is meant to facilitate balance rather than chaos. The statement does, however, appear to be an apt interpretation of Rangda, a symbol of the forces of chaos, and the delicate balance she holds with her opposite, Barong.

To continue with my analogies to Euro-North American popular culture, Rangda could also be said to be evocative of the male comedians in the Monty Python troupe playing one of their "Pepperpots," a series of ugly, crotchety, and occasionally violent old women. I will not venture to make too much of this comparison and, of course, make no claim of influence in either direction. However, in each case the performer is winkingly known by the audience to be male, while the character he is portraying is still read as female.

This does not alter the fact that Rangda and the Pepperpots function as caricatures of "bad women," but it does have strong implications for the degree to which women in general are viewed in this light. If the Rangda in the dance is a false woman, she is separated from real women and is not associated with them as one of the same kind. In fact, a woman is often called upon to play the part of a hero or a god in a dance-drama as, according to Judy Slattum, "few men have the ability to perform the exquisite qualities of a deity."[20] A similar arrangement is found in Monty Python where Carol Cleveland, the lone female performer, would never play the part of a Pepperpot but would often play a fresh-faced, pleasant young man.

Furthermore, while Rangda may be shown with a stylized mass of coarse, wild hair that is meant further to illustrate her similarly coarse, wild nature, this hair comes from an animal. This is naturally quite appropriate as yet another link between the witch and the bestial, but once again it shows us a false rather than a real woman. In contrast, the Barong's beard, such a sacred and potent part of the mask that it can be used to save entranced kris dancers from Rangda's spell, is made from the hair of a pre-menstruating girl.[21]

The construction of the masked Rangda cannot truly vilify women, because through being prevented from dancing the part they are not so closely connected with her. If women were viewed in such a negative light, it would be inconceivable for them to be asked not to play the villainous witch, but to play gods and heroes. It would be inconceivable that a girl's hair dipped in holy water could be a powerful antidote to black magic induced trance.

Rangda in the Work of Contemporary Women Artists in Bali

For a long time, the most notable characteristic of Rangda in the work of female visual artists in Bali was her absence. During my time in Ubud in 1999, I found no imagery of Rangda created by a woman artist, even when I visited Ubud's Seniwati Gallery of Art by Women, a gallery devoted to woman artists resident in Bali. When I asked Astri Wright, a professor at the University of Victoria who has done extensive research on contemporary Indonesian art, she did not at the time recall having seen any such works by Balinese women artists and only one by a woman, the Javanese artist Kartika Affandi, whom Wright has described as "the leading radical figure of the first generation of modern woman artists in Indonesia."[22] "Radical" is, indeed, an appropriate word for Kartika, who has never been afraid to tread her own path. To quote Wright again: "where women of her generation and class did not wear casual clothing in pubic in the 1980s, she did. Where others did not drive a van around, she did. While others would hesitate to study the axe-split head of a buffalo, she didn't."

Not only is Kartika unafraid of exploring the gruesome imagery of the buffalo head, but she has also tackled the subject of Rangda. In 1995, she painted *Dancer Stepping on My Head* (Plate 4), an image she identified to Wright as Rangda. Kartika later painted a more easily recognizable image of Rangda, but the 1995 work deals closely with how the witch struck her on a personal level. Although the palette used here is similar to Hendra Gunawan's painting, the color is applied in such as way as to express heightened tension. The paint comes straight from the tube, sometimes to be left in impasto swirls and streaks and sometimes to be smeared with the artist's fingers into solid blocks of color. Among the figures' distorted features it is possible to make out a dancer whose costume is adorned with severed heads and appendages that appear to represent the witch's long hair and characteristic necklace of human entrails. Underneath the dancer's raised foot is the artist's head, which may itself be severed or attached to a body already trampled into the ground. It is an image of horror and pain.

As Kartika was approaching the subject of Rangda as an Indonesian national but not a Balinese, it is difficult to know exactly what Rangda represents to her. Is her head being trampled in divine retribution for some past wrong-doing? Does she identify in some way with the victims in the story of Randeng Dirah? Perhaps Rangda symbolizes to Kartika a more abstract concept such as fear, anger, or hatred. The image may even function autobiographically, as a metaphor for the physical ailments that cause her discomfort and restrict her movement as the dancer does by pinning her down, or for the emotional pain she may feel at social stigma she faced for "presuming to become a modern artist" rather than following the accepted path of defining herself first and foremost as a wife and mother.[23] What is clear is that, as with the painting she did of a dead buffalo, Kartika approached this work as something challenging and difficult. It is challenging to the viewer in its violent and macabre subject matter and must have been even more so to the artist who chose to use such an image to express herself. I would argue that this willingness to paint difficult, potentially unpleasant subjects has drawn Kartika to paint Rangda when so many others have shied away from the image. It takes courage to invoke the Queen of the Witches.

It is possible that Balinese women artists chose not to depict Rangda because of a feeling of discomfort toward an unpleasant and unattractive subject. This was the basic interpretation taken by Mary Northmore, director of The Seniwati Gallery. She felt that Balinese artists prefer to paint cheerful, aesthetically pleasing subjects and tend to ignore the darker side. Even when the gallery had an exhibition of goddess images earlier in the 1990s, artists invariably chose to depict beautiful, benevolent goddesses such as Saraswati, Sita, or Dewi Sri. Sales are also bound to have an impact on artistic production, since most working artists cannot afford to paint subjects that past experience has proved will not sell. If the buying public, which often consists of affluent tourists, favors *legong* dancers, family scenes, and rice-fields, then artists will be more likely to explore these themes. This said, the encouragement of Balinese artists to paint according to foreign tastes can also work the other way. When asked about explorations by women artists in Bali of the darker side of Balinese mythology, Northmore could think of one artist, Suciarmi, who had painted Durga. She added that this was only done at the instigation of an American friend who was interested in the subject matter.

A short time after I left Bali, Javanese feminist poet Toeti Heraty published a book entitled *Kisah Perempuan Korban Patriarki* (2000), later released in English as *Calon Arang: The Story of a Woman Sacrificed to Patriarchy* (2006). In it, Heraty tells the story of the historical Rangda as a tale of women's oppression. As mentioned in Chapter 4, feminist reinterpretations of another culture can be problematic. Balinese playwright Cokorda Sawitri has noted that "Ibu Toeti is Javanese and is not referencing the historical and spiritual aspects of the story" and the Calonarang "in performance cannot be separated from its spiritual goals."[24] My reason for mentioning the book here is not to discuss its accuracy in the context of Balinese culture, as I believe that would be better served by a Balinese writer, but that it is illustrated with art by twenty-one different artists, all women and many Balinese.

As a group, illustrations for the book respond to both parts of its title. Some are visual interpretations of scenes from the Calonarang; others deal with the struggle faced by women in Indonesian society. Works with the latter theme present images such as a woman on her hands and knees, her head bowed as the red from the upper portion of the picture plane appears at once to bleed on her and press her down (*A Limited Independence* by Ni Ketut Ayu Sri Wardani), or *Recollection* by Ni Luh Nyoman Sri Rahayu that depicts a woman literally behind bars to show the lack of freedom she perceives in the lives of many women.

Of the works dealing specifically with the Calonarang, some, such as I Gusti Ayu Yasning's *Calon Arang in Balinese Tradition*, show just that. Rangda is instantly recognizable by her iconography and appears in the setting of a dance performance. Other works, however, approach the depiction of Rangda in very different way, exploring her human side as a loving mother. In *A Widow and Her Daughter*, Ni Putu Eni Astiarini wanted to show the deep bond between mother and daughter that would inspire the mother to make any sacrifice. She shows the widow as an older version of her beautiful daughter, leaning forward to take the girl's hand. I. G. P. A. Mirah Rahmawati also depicts the mother and daughter, but *The Treachery of a Daughter* shows a later moment in the story. Again, the loving, human mother stands protectively by the happy daughter, but here Ratna Mengali, newly married and blinded by love, will soon allow the sacred *lontar* to fall into the hands of her mother's enemies. The face of Rangda we are more accustomed to seeing appears, ghostly in the background, foreshadowing what is to come.

From Kartika's nightmare vision that tramples her underfoot to these images of a devoted mother whose only desire is to ensure her daughter's happiness, women artists have shown in their work how they personally respond and relate to the concept of Rangda. It is to be hoped that we can look forward to more such explorations of the different aspects of her character in the future.

Chapter 5

Conclusion

> Within the discourse on tourism and culture, "culture" has taken on a rarified status, as Balinese seek to identify for their interlocutors, tourists, academics, and development planners alike what is essentially Balinese. Thus the statements of identity convert readily into a set agenda of dance movements, or an elaborate ornamental carving style to be applied to the front of new public buildings and hotels alike. Within the discourse many Balinese have taken up positions that are opposite from the "tourism as a threat to culture" camp and argued that tourism reinforces Balinese culture.
>
> Adrian Vickers[1]

The Rangda Mask as Tourist Symbol

The impact of the interest by foreigners in Bali over the course of the past century cannot be overlooked. Tourists seek out those elements of culture in Bali that appear "exotic" in comparison to their native cultures, and those elements in turn become symbols that serve to encapsulate Balinese culture for the world. Thus Rangda, as an aspect of Balinese "statements of identity," is converted into a memorable image on book covers and postcards through which Balinese cultural tourism is marketed.

Above I referred to an anecdote told to me by Murni in which her non-Balinese boyfriend expressed an interest in capturing a record of Rangda's appearance. While Murni was terrified, he was thinking of photo opportunities. The reaction of Murni's boyfriend to Rangda is not unusual for people from outside of Bali. Visitors to the island are just as intrigued by the image of the Queen of the Witches now as they were in Walter Spies's day. One of the things that struck me during my time in Bali was the proliferation of images of Rangda. In addition to the many performances of

Conclusion

the Calonarang put on exclusively for tourists (as opposed to serving any specific religious function), she could be found both in the form of masks, full scale and miniature, created for sale to tourists and as printed pictures on the covers of any number of books written for the tourist market (Fig. 9). Presented to visitors in this fashion, as one of the key images in Balinese culture, Rangda becomes a symbol of Bali. Given this is meant to be the same being that the tourist pamphlets hail as "the evil, hair-raising witch, a symbol of villainy, hatred, lust, jealousy, and everything else that's nasty," I found myself extremely curious what Balinese made of this seemingly unlikely choice of cultural emblem. Thus, the last question I posed in each interview involved attempted to discover whether and the extent to which each informant found Rangda an acceptable image to present to the world as synonymous with Bali.

Figure 9. Rangda masks for sale, Ubud

Even with such a small sampling of individuals as I had to work with, I was surprised at the range of opinions on the subject. Agung Rai felt it was entirely appropriate for the mask of Rangda to serve as the face of Bali because for him, Rangda is the symbol of the balance between good and bad, and this balance is,

The Rangda Mask as Tourist Symbol

in turn, indicative of Bali Hindu cosmology. The *balian* and the teacher I spoke with both condoned the practice, but added the qualifier that it was necessary for people to distinguish between the Rangda encountered in a shop window versus the Rangda prayed to in a temple. The masks made for foreign consumption in the image of Rangda are not made of sacred wood and have been subjected to none of the rituals that would allow them to be filled with divine energy. That said, it is not entirely unheard of for masks made for the tourist market to become charged with magic power. As Judy Slattum was told by a former director of the Art Center of Bali, "If you make an attractive home, someone will want to live in it."[2] Since this is a rare occurrence, however, the vast majority of these masks, not containing the spirit of Rangda, are seen to have little in common with the real Rangda as she appears through sacred masks. Both the *balian* and the teacher felt that as long as this distinction was understood, there was no problem in using the image of Rangda as a symbol of Bali. Both said they were happy that people from other parts of the world were interested in Rangda, as this demonstrated an interest in Bali Hindu culture. In their eyes, Rangda is a means of promoting that culture.

The *pedanda* I Ketut Arthana partly agreed with this, in that he was pleased to see that "Most people in the world know about Balinese culture." He did, however, have one objection to the situation: he was not convinced that all visitors to Bali would make the distinction between the two Rangdas. "As Balinese, we are scared that people don't really understand—maybe they think the Rangda in the art shop and the Rangda in the temple are the same." To consider the physical form of Rangda as it appears in a commercial setting, without regard to ceremony, to be inherently synonymous with the powerful Queen of the Witches who can protect the people or spread illness at will would be quite blasphemous in the context of the Balinese religion.

Arthana does well to be worried, for it is unlikely that the bulk of tourists, most of whom have only seen non-sacred Calonarang performances put on for their viewing pleasure, have any concept of the complexity of Rangda's character. As Belo wrote in *Bali: Rangda and Barong*, Rangda "has the sort of authenticity that in our culture belongs to Santa Claus, to the Tax Collector, and to the Angel of Death—with the difference that we could not very well imagine all these figures rolled into one, while the Balinese find no difficulty attributing to Rangda such a multiplicity."[3]

Not only are we unaccustomed to collapsing many characteristics into one entity within the context of Euro-North American culture, but there is also a tendency to treat figures from other cultures similarly. A children's book by the

Conclusion

Australian writer Stephanie Owen Reeder illustrated by Javanese installation artist Dadang Christanto is a case in point. *The Flaming Witch* deals with the story of the historical Rangda and her battle with Mpu Baradah. Described in a panel on the back cover as a new translation from the Old Javanese by the author, the story is not noticeably different from the account of the historical Rangda presented here. There is a difference, however, that lies not in narrative structure but in the many layers of meaning behind the story. According to the book's back cover, "Rangda is a powerful witch, and she is angry enough to bring down a curse on the whole kingdom. This beautiful, peaceful kingdom where no one is hungry and no one is poor is suddenly a place of fire and destruction."[4] True, this is one aspect of Rangda and what she is capable of, but the writer goes on to say that the story presented in *The Flaming Witch* is still performed today. As a result, parents and children who are introduced to Rangda via this book will not think that the Calonarang dance is about maintaining cosmic balance, or that Rangda can be called a goddess, or that she can be a protective force. The resulting misunderstanding appears to be the literary equivalent to the *pedanda*'s concern that the visitors confronted with Rangda masks in shop windows will be under the impression that what they see is synonymous with the sacred image of Rangda.

For Pak and Ibu Agung, there was little question of Rangda's being a good choice for a symbol of Bali. Ibu Agung was simply uncomfortable with the prevalence of such a frightening image and the idea that people from outside Bali would associate the island and its culture with Rangda: "Already, people say 'Oh, Rangda—magic.'" Pak Agung did not like the idea of using Rangda as a symbol of Bali any more than his wife did. For him however, Rangda did not conjure up images of terror, as he thought of the darker forces as something not to be feared so much as understood and respected, but rather of anger and aggression: "Yes, I do mind," he said. "If Rangda is to be a symbol of Bali, because there are a lot of things possible in Bali, because," he joked. "Bali is pretty cute." Growing serious again, he added, "But Rangda is like a monster. Rangda is good for a symbol of anger. If we were to use Rangda as a symbol of Bali, Bali would be [seen as] very strong and aggressive. But, as you know, people in Bali are not really aggressive. That [Rangda] is the symbol when people are angry."

As can be seen from even these few responses, there are any number of different and highly individual views on the way in which the mask of Rangda is presented to the world. Why choose Rangda as a cultural symbol when there are so many mixed feelings on the part of the Balinese about the selection? Certainly no referenda have been held on the subject. To Rucina Ballinger, the choice is clearly related to the taste for the "exotic" and sensational that so often intrigues people from one culture when presented with a different one: "To sell books or a culture, one must choose something exotic, and you can't get much more exotic than a witch who makes people go into trance." That turning Bali into a magical mystery tour through the presentation of Rangda still attracts visitors today makes one wonder if perceptions have changed much since Spies and Co. were first intrigued by the darker side of paradise in the 1930s. As Vickers writes: "It may not be true to say that 'paradise hasn't changed in a thousand years' [as the tourist books and pamphlets are fond of doing], but it is true to say that tourist images have not changed in over fifty years. The only difference is that Indonesians, not Europeans, must take credit for these statements and images."[5]

I would argue that there is no single, unified, typically Balinese response to Rangda in contemporary society. Perhaps there never was. Context and venue may be highly influential as well, as the teacher from Tabanan suggested with regards to the notion that what is terrifying by torchlight may be less so by fluorescent light. In addition, it is worth mentioning that I interviewed the teacher in a courtyard behind an auto repair garage where vehicles were being worked on while we spoke, while Agung Rai was interviewed on the grounds of ARMA where we were surrounded by architecture and sculpture in a traditional style. Is it possible that an individual's view on whether Rangda's power is still pervasive or whether she is being slowly but surely ousted by the influx of Western technology and culture could be subtly influenced by their location, either in a mechanics' workshop surrounded by Japanese cars and motorbikes or in an art museum surrounded by examples of traditional Balinese art?

Throughout this book I have stressed the multiplicity of meanings that may be associated with Rangda. The personal views of Balinese, both my own contacts and those of past researchers, have played an important part in this approach. Is it possible, though, to avoid generalizations altogether? I would unfortunately have to argue that it is not. The logistics, as has been said earlier, are prohibitive: realistically, one cannot interview *everyone* and hope to include all the findings in a single written work. Researchers must be content to collect as much data as they can and make projections beyond that. In practical terms, the majority comes to stand for the whole. Even when focusing on a small number of individuals as in this book, and presenting the information accordingly, it is impossible to avoid the fact that the informants themselves may be inclined to essentialize their culture. By way of example, I remind the reader of these statements by informants:

Conclusion

"In Bali, we believe that when the good spirits are well disposed toward someone, the bad spirits will never disturb [that person]."

– *Pemangku*

"People are always scared [of Rangda]."

– Agung Rai

"All people want to get married."

– Ibu Agung

There is no small irony in the fact that these essentializing statements come from the very people whose multiplicity I had been seeking to present. There is a difference, however, between the way in which people may represent their culture and the way that it is appropriate for an outsider to do so. In one case it is simply an observation; in the other it is often seen as a stereotype. In the case of Bali, observations made by outsiders throughout the last century have too often been privileged over those made by Balinese. The unequal positions of power for the researcher and the researched makes it all the more important for the former to endeavor to avoid essentializing Balinese culture . . . even when the researcher's informants are doing precisely that.

Rangda in Discourses Outside Bali: 1930s to the Present

During the early part of the last century, scholars were not yet addressing the notion of "power over" with the self-reflexivity that has characterized more and more recent writing that seeks to cross cultures. Then, a Rangda mask would evoke images of a moonlit temple courtyard filled with the heady aroma of incense and the shouts of men going into trance, or tiny flickering blue lights floating down a deserted path as *leyak* roamed the village byways—in short, an image like that found in Spies's capture of Rangda at a Barong dance. This description of a hypothetical thought association is indicative of the romantic approach to Balinese culture alluded to in Chapter 1.

A more critical anthropological discourse was created by Bateson, Mead, and later Belo, but this approach was strongly colored by those scholars' interest in Freudian theories. As Lansing wrote in *Evil in the Morning of the World*, "while many of Belo's observations are illuminating, the ultimate meaning that she attaches to the ceremony may have more to do with the *Weltanschauung* of the early Freudian anthropologists of the thirties than with that of the Balinese."[6]

Rangda in Discourses Outside Bali: 1930s to the Present

When anthropologists such as the Clifford Geertz began undertaking their studies on Bali in the 1960s, they attempted to take a less enraptured, more respectful approach to the culture than was evident in the work of Covarrubias, and less psychoanalytically based than Mead's. This was continued by the next generation of anthropologists in the late 1980s and the early 1990s, with studies done by Vickers, Wikan, Barth, and others. These works added much to the study of Bali, but less to the study of Rangda.

Hence, little has been produced that deals especially with the figure of Rangda. *Bali: Rangda and Barong* has unfortunately become outdated. For one thing, the author's close connection with Margaret Mead (who had encouraged her to write the book) led her to approach Rangda through a predominantly psychoanalytic filter, an approach that has fallen out of favor in recent years when taken as an interpretation to be privileged above all others. Belo's book is also outdated simply because its publication date of roughly sixty years ago makes it unable to address the affect of newer technologies and the influx of foreign cultures on the mythology of the island. The individuals Belo may have interviewed or observed did not have to explain how they felt about the images of Rangda staring at them row upon row from the covers of books or videos in all the languages of the "First World." They did not sit in auto repair shops while considering the detrimental effects of improved access to electricity on the younger generation's belief in old stories. They were not approached for interviews in internet cafés designed for an international community or observed during dance performances staged nightly for large audiences composed wholly of tourists.

I am not attempting with these examples to conjure up an image of a culture eroded by over fifty years of ever-increasing tourism. The Ubud Pura Dalem was undergoing restoration while I was there, a process that included cleaning or replacing some of the smaller statues as needed. I came across a place where some of these statues were temporarily being stored and found old and new Rangdas (Fig. 10), some standing side by side. Even the traditional imagery of Rangda in a most traditional context continues to be present and in a constant state of renewal. I will suggest, however, that the relationship between many people in Bali and Rangda has changed over time due to the new issues brought about by the influence of technology or by concessions made to foreigners so that they might feel reasonably at home. These issues add yet another layer to the multiple incarnations and interpretations of Rangda.

In this book I have attempted to present a few of the aspects of Rangda's complex nature that have thus far not found their way into any single study of her. Why this

Conclusion

Figure 10. Temporary storage in Ubud Pura Dalem

has not occurred previously is a question well worth asking. Perhaps it is because she does not fit easily into any single field of study, calling instead for an interdisciplinary approach that draws upon art history, anthropology, and religious studies. Also, if we consider, as many do, *Bali: Rangda and Barong* to be the definitive study of Rangda in that this has been the only monograph to be dedicated to the subject, we must take into account the influence of that period on the nature of the study. The multiplicity allowed by postmodernism's emphasis on pluralism seems quite natural now, but writers from previous eras were not necessarily encouraged to approach topics in this way. In a time when an open-ended study would seem an unfinished one, it was appropriate for Belo to conclude her monograph by saying that "Rangda, in her connection with death, destruction, and disease, is but the ugly counterpart of living, procreation, and well being."[7]

I might well have had difficulty presenting my work in an earlier era, for if asked to answer "Who or what is Rangda?" in a single statement, I would initially have to respond with the open-ended statement: "She is many things." Fortunately, the present time allows more room for "both and" rather than strictly "either or" interpretations, as well as a greater capacity for paradox and contradiction. This is an approach that works well for Rangda, allowing as it does for many non-mutually exclusive readings that reflect the many overlapping identities she holds in the culture of Bali, both traditional Hindu and what might be called "modern international." Thus, Rangda may both be a threat to *and* a protector of the village, a force of chaos *and* a defender of order.

As a final illustration of Rangda's multiple identities, I return once more to *Barong I*, the painting by Hendra Gunawan introduced at the beginning of this book. We can see how Rangda simultaneously threatens to explode the picture plan with her wild dancing and watches over the human community below. The latter appears to be a protective gesture if one looks at the unconcern displayed by the people in the mid-ground. Hendra paints her with the distinctive facial features that we have come to associate with Rangda, but it is impossible to tell whether the artist is depicting a dancer wearing a mask or the face of the goddess herself. As in the context of the sacred dance where even a dancer wearing the Rangda mask is never simply a dancer in a costume, there is no reason why it cannot be both things at once.

We may ask who Rangda is doing battle with here. Is she preparing for the next round of a fight with Barong who waits among the members of the human community? Does her position far from the community's activities present an example to women who would allow themselves to be similarly outcast by remaining unmarried? Is she magically causing illness to the people in the painting or to the people outside the picture plane? Or, are we seeing her in the act of chasing off an evil spirit that stands behind the viewer's shoulder? She has the capacity to do all these things.

It is not necessary, nor has it been the intent of this book, to suggest that Rangda as a cultural and religious entity is simply all things to all people. She does, indeed, have many identities that may come into play in a variety of contexts, but these identities overlap in that they share a common root or purpose. As the most powerful conduit of black magic in Bali, Rangda is akin to the black squares in the sacred *poleng* cloth that often adorns her statues: she is a vital component of the duality that ultimately makes up the whole. When one considers, as some of my informants did, that magical power is inherently neither good nor bad, then Rangda is not only a force of black magic opposed to white magic. One could say that she is ultimately a conduit of power that exists beyond the terms bad or good.

The idea of expanding and collapsing identities that permeates Bali Hindu cosmology can also be applied to Rangda. As with the entity called Sanghyang Widi Wasa, who may be infinitely divided to express each characteristic of divinity

Conclusion

in Bali, Rangda is the Queen of the Witches who contains within her all the identities discussed here and many more besides. Her complexity arises not only from variations in context and function, but also from the way in which these variations combine to form a whole. This whole cannot be properly understood, however, without an awareness of the many parts that create it. And, without recognizing the complexity of these parts, the whole would be considerably less rich.

Notes

Introduction

[1] Full bibliographical details, including sub-titles, for the references below are to be found in the List of Works Cited. Below, an author's full name appears only on first use; thereafter reference is by surname. John Stephen Lansing, *Evil in the Morning of the World*, p. 75.
[2] Adrian Vickers, *Bali*, pp. 105–07.
[3] Lansing, *Evil in the Morning of the World*, pp. 74–76; Vickers, *Bali*, p. 123.
[4] Hildred Geertz, *Images of Power*, p. 81.
[5] From a pamphlet accompanying *wayang kulit* performances by Made Gender in Ubud, summer 1999.
[6] Willard A. Hanna, *Bali Profile*, p. 135.
[7] Lansing, *Evil in the Morning of the World*, p. 75.
[8] Clifford Geertz, "'Native's Point of View'" in *Local Knowledge*, p. 58.
[9] Jane Belo, *Bali*, p. 19.
[10] James A. Boon, *Affinities and Extremes*, p. 90; Miguel Covarrubias, *Island of Bali*, p. 88.
[11] Unni Wikan, *Managing Turbulent Hearts*, p. xv.
[12] Lansing, *Evil in the Morning of the World*, p. 75.
[13] Mark Hobart, "Introduction" in Hobart and Taylor, eds., *Context, Meaning, and Power in Southeast Asia*, p. 8.

Chapter 1
Situating Rangda in Past Discourses

[1] C. Hooykaas, *Religion in Bali*, p.1.
[2] Vickers, *Bali*, p.126.

Notes

[3] Belo, *Bali*, p.285.
[4] Gregory Bateson and Margaret Mead, *Balinese Character*, pp. 34–35.
[5] Belo, *Bali*, p. 38.
[6] Frank Cioffi "Was Freud a Liar" in *Unauthorized Freud*, p. 34.
[7] Bateson and Mead, *Balinese Character*, p. 36.
[8] Barbara Lovric, "Bali: Myth, Magic, and Morbidity" in *Death and Disease in Southeast Asia*, p. 139.
[9] Brian Bell, ed., *Insight Guides: Bali*, p. 91.
[10] Lansing, *Evil in the Morning of the World*, p. 81.

Chapter 2
Rangda's Singular Appearance and Multiple Identities

[1] *Ibid.*, p. 75.
[2] Walter Spies and Beryl DeZoete, *Dance and Drama in Bali*, p. 2.
[3] Clifford Geertz, "Deep Play: Notes on the Balinese Cockfight" in *The Interpretation of Cultures*, p. 417.
[4] Lansing, *Evil in the Morning of the World*, p. 2.
[5] Belo, "Trance Experience in Bali" in *Ritual, Play, and Performance*, pp. 159, 161.
[6] Belo, *Bali*, p. 32.
[7] David Napier, *Masks, Transformation, and Paradox*, pp. 206–20.
[8] Lovric, "Bali," pp. 117–41.
[9] Geertz, *Images of Power*, p. 16.
[10] Colin McPhee, "The Balinese *Wayang Kulit* and its Music" in Belo, *Bali*, p. 182.
[11] Hooykaas, *Religion in Bali*, p. 1.
[12] Judy Slattum, *Masks of Bali*, pp. 124–27.
[13] Michele Stephen, *Desire, Divine and Demonic: Balinese Mysticism in the Paintings of I Ketut Budiana and I Gusti Nyoman Mirdiana*, p. 81.
[14] Belo, *Bali*, p. 20.
[15] Hobart, Ramseyer, and Leeman, *The Peoples of Bali*, p. 198.
[16] Belo, *Bali*, p. 19.
[17] Hobart, Ramseyer, and Leeman, p. 178.
[18] C. Hooykaas, *Drawings of Balinese Sorcery*, p. 14.
[19] Kristi Ross, "The Barong and Rangda," *Parabola*, p. 79.
[20] David R. Kinsley, *Hindu Goddesses*, p. 118.
[21] Hooykaas, *Drawings of Balinese Sorcery*, p. 7.

Notes

Chapter 3
Truly Evil or Not?: Philosophical and Ethical Dimensions of Rangda

[1] Lansing, *Evil in the Morning of the World*, p. 81.
[2] *Webster's II New Riverside Dictionary*, 1984.
[3] Angela Hobart, *Healing Performances of Bali*, p. 130.
[4] Wikan, *Managing Turbulent Hearts*, p. 6.
[5] Belo, *Bali*, p. 18.
[6] Wikan, *Managing Turbulent Hearts*, p. 248.
[7] *Ibid.*

Chapter 4
Implications of Rangda for Constructing the Feminine

[1] Margot Miffin, "Feminism's New Face" cited in Joanna Frueh, Cassandra Langer, and Arlene Raven, eds., *New Feminist Criticism*, p. 200.
[2] Margo Machida, "(re)-Orienting," *Ibid.*, p. 178.
[3] Hartley Productions, *Bali: Mask of Rangda*.
[4] Geertz, *Images of Power*, pp. 70, 16.
[5] Unni Wikan, *Managing Turbulent Hearts*, p. 86.
[6] *Ibid.*, p. 43.
[7] *Ibid.*, p. 11.
[8] Kaja McGowan, "Balancing on Bamboo," *Asian Art and Culture*, p. 77.
[9] Francine Rainone and Janice Moulton, "Sex Roles and the Sexual Division of Labor" in *"Femininity," "Masculinity," and "Androgyny,"* p. 233.
[10] Wikan, *Managing Turbulent Hearts*, p. xvii.
[11] *Ibid.*, p. 28.
[12] McGowan, "Balancing on Bamboo" p. 87.
[13] Slattum, *Masks of Bali*, p. 72.
[14] Hooykaas, *Drawings of Balinese Sorcery*, p. 195.
[15] Covarrubias, *Island of Bali*, pp. 332, 356.
[16] Francine Brinkgreve, "The Cili and Other Female Images in Bali" in Elsbeth Locher-Scholten and Anke Niehof, eds., *Indonesian Women in Focus*, pp. 136–41.
[17] Angela Hobart, *Healing Performances of Bali*, p. 165.
[18] *Ibid.*, p. 127.
[19] Mircea Eliade *Mephistopheles and the Androgyne*, pp. 112–14, cited in O'Flaherty, *Women, Androgynes, and Other Mythical Beasts*, p. 297.

Notes

[20] Slattum, *Masks of Bali*, p. 19.
[21] Hobart, *Healing Performances of Bali*, p.144.
[22] Astri Wright, "Self-taught against the Grain" in May Datuin Flaudette, ed., *Woman Imaging Women*, p. 11.
[23] *Ibid.*
[24] Rucina Ballinger, *Calon Arang*.

Chapter 5
Conclusion

[1] Adrian Vickers, *Being Modern in Bali*, pp. 27–28.
[2] Slattum, *Masks of Bali*, p. 14.
[3] Belo, *Bali*, p. 19.
[4] Stephanie Owen Reeder, *The Flaming Witch*: back cover.
[5] Vickers, *Bali*, p.192.
[6] Lansing, *Evil in the Morning of the World*, p. 77.
[7] Belo, *Bali*, p. 59.

Glossary of Balinese Terms

Agama Hindu Dharma The Balinese form of Hinduism, characterized by the desire to preserve balance between all the opposing forces composing the world

Balian Traditional healer and magician

Barong Supernatural creature representing the forces of good; can take many forms but commonly found as the lion-like Barong Ket; sometimes used as the name of the dance in which Barong battles Rangda

Calonarang The story of the historical Rangda; performed as a dance-drama a powerful exorcism rite culminating in Rangda's battle against Barong

Dewi Sri Bali Hindu goddess of rice, also known as the Rice Mother

Durga Warrior aspect of Devi, the Great Goddess

Kali "The Dark One"; the ferocious aspect of the Great Goddess

Kris Sacred dagger; used by entranced dancers to attempt to attack Rangda in the Calonarang dance

Leyak Person who has studied black magic and uses it destructively

Lontar Sacred text written on bound palm leaves

Mahendradatta An eleventh-century Javanese princess said to be the historical Rangda

Mpu Baradah The holy man who challenged Rangda to a sorcerer's duel

Pedanda High priest of the Brahmin caste

Pemangku Family or village priest, generally from the Sudra caste

Glossary of Balinese Terms

Poleng Black-and-white checked cloth symbolizing the balance of opposing forces
Pura Dalem Temple of the Dead, associated with Siwa and Durga
Pura Desa Village temple; associated with Wisnu

Randeng Dirah "The widow of Dirah," Dirah being a province in East Java; another name for the historical Rangda
Ratna Mengali Mahendradatta's beautiful daughter
Rawana Demon king and villain of the *Ramayana*

Sakti Magical power
Sanghyang Widi Wasa The ultimate deity, of whom all Balinese gods are a manifestation

Tenget Sacred; imbued with divine power
Trimurti A trinity of the gods: Brahma (the Creator), Wisnu (the Preserver), and Siwa (the Destroyer)

Works Cited

Aiyar, Indira S. *Durga as Mahisasuramardini: A Dynamic Myth of Goddess.* New Delhi: Gyan Publishing House, 1997.
Ballinger, Rucina. "Calon Arang: A New Context for an Old Witch." <www.saritaksu.com/ca-launch.html> [*Jakarta Post*, 5 November 2006].
Bandem, I Madé, and Fredrik deBoer. *Balinese Dance in Transition, Kaja and Kelod.* Kuala Lumpur: Oxford University Press, 1995.
Barth, Fredrik. *Balinese Worlds.* Chicago: University of Chicago Press, 1993.
Bateson, Gregory, and Margaret Mead. *Balinese Character: A Photographic Analysis.* New York: New York Academy of Sciences, 1942.
Bell, Brian, ed., *Insight Guides: Bali.* 15th edn. London: Apa Publications, 1970; rpt. 1997.
Belo, Jane. *Bali: Rangda and Barong.* Seattle: University of Washington Press, 1949; rpt. 1966.
Belo, Jane. *Trance in Bali.* New York: Columbia University Press, 1960.
Belo, Jane ed. *Traditional Balinese Culture.* New York: Columbia University Press, 1970.
Berkson, Carmel. *The Divine and the Demonic: Mahisa's Heroic Struggle with Durga.* Delhi: Oxford University Press, 1995.
Boon, James A. *Affinities and Extremes: Crisscrossing the Bittersweet Ethnology of East Indies History, Hindu-Balinese Culture, and Indo-European Allure.* Chicago: University of Chicago Press, 1990.
Brinkgreve, Francine. "The Cili and Other Female Images in Bali." In Elsbeth Locher-Scholten and Anke Niehof, eds., *Indonesian Women in Focus: Past and Present Notions.* Leiden: KITLV Press, 1992, pp.135–51.
Cabezón, José Ignacio. "Mother Wisdom, Father Love: Gender-based Imagery in Mahayana Buddhist Thought." In José Ignacio Cabezón, ed., *Buddhism, Sexuality, and Gender.* New York: State University of New York Press, 1992, pp. 181–99.

Works Cited

Cahill, Tim. "The Entranced Duck Always Gets the Laugh: Adrift in Bali, Quacking against the Current of Time." *Outside*, 34.1 (1 January 1999): 39–42.

Coburn, Thomas B. "Consort of None, Sakti of All: The Vision of the Devi- mahatmya." In John Stratton Hawley and Donna Marie Wulf, eds., *The Divine Consort: Radha and the Goddesses of India*. Berkeley and Delhi: Berkeley Graduate Theological Union and Motilal Banarsidass Publishers, 1982, pp.153–65.

Coedès, G. *The Indianized States of Southeast Asia*. Honolulu: East-West Center Press, 1964; rpt. 1968.

Connor. Linda. "Corpse Abuse and Trance in Bali: The Cultural Mediation of Aggression." *Mankind*, 12 (1979): 104–18.

Covarrubias, Miguel. *Island of Bali*. New York: Knopf, 1937.

Crews, Frederick, ed. *Unauthorized Freud: Doubters Confront a Legend*. New York: Penguin-Putnam, 1998.

Dibia, I Wayan, and Rucina Ballinger. *Balinese Dance, Drama, and Music: A Guide to the Performing Arts of Bali*. Singapore: Periplus Editions, 2004.

Edge, Hoyt. "Possession in Two Balinese Trance Ceremonies." *Anthropology of Consciousness*, 7.4 (1996): 1–8.

Eiseman, Fred B., Jr., *Woodcarvings of Bali*. Berkeley: Periplus Editions, 1988.

Eiseman, Fred B., Jr., and Margaret Eiseman. *Bali: Sekala and Niskala, Volume I: Essays on Religion, Ritual, and Art*. Jakarta: Periplus Editions, 1990.

Eiseman, Fred B., Jr., and Margaret Eiseman. *Bali: Sekala and Niskala, Volume II: Essays on Society, Tradition, and Craft*. Berkeley: Periplus Editions, 1990.

Feuerstein, George. *Tantra: The Path of Ecstasy*. Boston: Shambhala, 1998.

Frueh, Joanna, Cassandra L. Langer, and Arlene Raven, eds. *New Feminist Criticism: Art, Identity, Action*. New York: Icon Editions, 1994.

Geertz, Clifford. *Person, Time, and Conduct in Bali: An Essay in Cultural Analysis*. New Haven, Connecticut: Yale University Press, 1966.

Geertz, Clifford. *The Interpretation of Cultures*. New York: Basic Books, 1973.

Geertz, Clifford. *Local Knowledge: Further Essays in Interpretive Anthropology*. New York: Basic Books, 1983.

Geertz, Hildred. *Images of Power: Balinese Painting made for Gregory Bateson and Margaret Mead*. Honolulu: University of Hawaii Press, 1994.

Haks, F., Leo Haks, Jop Ubbens, Adrian Vickers, and Guus Maris. *Pre-war Balinese Modernists, 1928–1942: An Additional Page in Art History*. Haarlem, Netherlands: Ars et Animato, 1999.

Hanna, Willard A. *Bali Profile: People, Events, Circumstances, 1001–1976*. New York: American Universities Field Staff, 1976.

Works Cited

Hartley Productions. *Bali, Mask of Rangda*. Cos Cob, Connecticut: Hartley Film Foundation, 1974.
Hefner, Robert W. *Hindu Javanese: Tengger Tradition and Islam*. Princeton, New Jersey: Princeton University Press, 1985.
Heraty, Toeti. *Calon Arang: The Story of a Woman Sacrificed to Patriarchy*. Sanur: Saritaksu Editions, 2006.
Hobart, Angela. *Dancing Shadows of Bali: Theatre and Myth*. London: KPI, 1987.
Hobart, Angela. *Healing Performances of Bali: Between Darkness and Light*. New York: Berghahn Books, 2003.
Hobart, Angela, Urs Ramseyer, and Albert Leeman. *The Peoples of Bali*. Oxford: Blackwell Publishers, 1996.
Hobart. Mark. "The Path of the Soul: The Legitimacy of Nature in Balinese Conceptions of Space." In G. B. Milner, ed., *Natural Symbols in South East Asia*. School of Oriental and African Studies, University of London, 1978, pp. 5–28.
Höfer, Hans, director. *Insight Guides: Bali*. London: APA Publications, 1970; rpt. 1997.
Holt, Claire. *Art in Indonesia: Continuities and Change*. Ithaca, New York: Cornell University Press, 1967.
Hooykaas, C. *Religion in Bali*. Leiden: Brill, 1973.
Hooykaas, C. *Drawings of Balinese Sorcery*. Leiden: Brill, 1980.
Hospital, Clifford, *The Riteous Demon: A Study of Bali*. Vancouver: University of British Columbia Press, 1984.
Kinsley, David R. "Blood and Death out of Place: Reflections on the Goddess Kali." In John Stratton Hawley and Donna Marie Wulf, eds., *The Divine Consort: Radha and the Goddesses of India*. Berkeley and Delhi: Berkeley Graduate Theological Union/ Motilal Banarsidass Publishers, 1982, pp. 144–52.
Kinsley, David R. *Hindu Goddesses: Visions of the Divine Feminine in the Hindu Religious Tradition*. Berkeley: University of California Press, 1986; rpt. 1988.
Kinsley, David R. *The Goddesses' Mirror: Visions of the Divine from East and West*. New York: State University of New York Press, 1989.
Lansing, John Stephen. *Evil in the Morning of the World: Phenomenological Approaches to a Balinese Community*. Ann Arbor: University of Michigan Center for South and Southeast Asian Studies, 1974.
Lansing, John Stephen. *The Three Worlds of Bali*. Washington, DC: PBS Video, 1981.
Lansing, John Stephen. *Priests and Programmers: Technologies of Power in the Engineered Landscape of Bali*. Princeton, New Jersey: Princeton University Press, 1991.
Lovric, Barbara. "Bali: Myth, Magic and Morbidity." In Norman Owen, ed., *Death and Disease in Southeast Asia: Explorations in Social, Medical, and Demographic History*.

Works Cited

Singapore: Oxford University Press, 1987, pp. 117–41.

McGowan, Kaja Maria. "Balancing on Bamboo: Women in Balinese Art." *Asian Art and Culture*, 8.1 (1995): 74–95.

Maquet, Jacques. *The Aesthetic Experience: An Anthropologist Looks at Art*. New Haven, Connecticut: Yale University Press, 1986.

Matsui, Yayori. *Women's Asia*. London: Zed Books, 1989.

Moor, Edward. *The Hindu Pantheon*. Varanasi and Delhi: Indological Book House, 1810; rev. edn. 1968.

Nabholz-Kartaschoff, Marie-Louise. "A Sacred Cloth of Rangda: Kamben Cepuk of Bali and Nusa Penida." In Mattibelle Gittenger, ed., *To Speak with Cloth: Studies in Indonesian Textiles*. Los Angeles: Museum of Cultural History, University of California, 1989, pp. 181–98.

Napier, David A. *Masks, Transformation, and Paradox*. Berkeley: University of California Press, 1986.

Nochlin, Linda. *Women, Art, and Power and Other Essays*. New York: Harper & Row, 1988.

O'Flaherty, Wendy Doniger. *The Origins of Evil in Hindu Mythology*. Berkeley: University of California Press, 1976.

O'Flaherty, Wendy Doniger. *Women, Androgynes, and Other Mythical Beasts*. Chicago: University of Chicago Press, 1980.

Ottin, Meery, and Alban Bensa. *Le Sacré à Java et à Bali: Chamanisme, sorcellerie et transe*. Paris: Robert Laffont, 1969.

Owen Reader, Stephanie, and Dadang Christanto. *The Flaming Witch*. Sydney: Random House Australia, 1997.

Poebatjaraka, R. M. Ng. "De Calon Arang" *Bijdragen tot de Taal-, Land-, en Volkenkunde*, 82 (1926): 110–86.

Robinson, Geoffrey. *The Dark Side of Paradise: Political Violence in Bali*. Ithaca, New York: Cornell University Press, 1995.

Ross, Kristi. "The Barong and Rangda: Balancing the Opposites in the Balinese World." *Parabola*, 28.3 (2003): 78–84.

Sears, Laurie J., ed. *Fantasizing the Feminine in Indonesia*. Durham, North Carolina: Duke University Press, 1996.

Shah, Idries Sayed. *Oriental Magic*. London: Octagon Press, 1956; rpt. 1968.

Sharma, Arvind, ed. *Women in World Religions*. New York: State University of New York Press, 1987.

Slattum, Judy. *Masks of Bali: Spirits of an Ancient Drama*. San Francisco: Chronicle Books, 1992.

Works Cited

Soemantri, Hilda, Jim Supangkat, and Jean Couteau, eds. *Indonesian Heritage—Visual Art.* Singapore: Archipelago Press, 1998.

Spies, Walter, and Beryl de Zoete. *Dance and Drama in Bali.* London: Faber & Faber, 1938; rpt. 1973.

Steinburg, David Joel, ed. *In Search of Southeast Asia: A Modern History.* Honolulu: University of Hawaii Press, 1971; rev. edn. 1985.

Stephen, Michele. *Desire, Divine and Demonic: Balinese Mysticism in the Paintings of I Ketut Budiana and I Gusti Nyoman Mirdiana.* Honolulu, University of Hawaii Press, 2005.

Storey, John. "Feminism." In *An Introduction to Cultural Theory and Popular Culture.* 2nd edn. Athens, Georgia: University of Georgia Press, 1998.

Suradaya, I Nyoman. Pamphlet distributed by the Pura Desa Ubud for the Temple Anniversary of 25–28 July 1999.

Tantri, K'tut. *Revolt in Paradise.* Jakarta: Gramedia Publishing Division, 1981.

Vaudeville, Charlotte. "Krishna Gopala, Radha, and The Great Goddess." In John Stratton Hawley and Donna Marie Wulf, eds., *The Divine Consort: Radha and the Goddesses of India.* Berkeley and Delhi: Berkeley Graduate Theololgical Union/ Motilal Banarsidass Publishers, 1982, pp. 1–12.

Vickers, Adrian. *Bali: A Paradise Created.* Singapore: Periplus Editions, 1989.

Vickers, Adrian, ed. *Being Modern in Bali: Image and Change.* New Haven, Connecticut: Yale University Press, 1996.

Wakefield, Neville. *Postmodernism: The Twilight of the Real.* London: Pluto Press, 1990.

Warming, Wanda, and Michael Gaworski. *The World of Indonesian Textiles.* London: Serinda Publications, 1981.

Wertheim, W. F., ed., *Bali: Studies in Life, Thought, and Ritual.* The Hague and Bandung: W. Van Hoeve, 1960.

Wiener, Margaret J. *Visible and Invisible Realms: Power, Magic, and Colonial Conquest in Bali.* Chicago: University of Chicago Press, 1995.

Wikan, Unni. "Public Grace and Private Fears: Gaiety, Offense, and Sorcery in North Bali." *Ethos*, 15 (1987): 337–65.

Wikan, Unni. *Managing Turbulent Hearts: A Balinese Formula for Living.* Chicago: University of Chicago Press, 1990.

Wright, Astri. *Soul, Spirit, and Mountain: Preoccupations of Contemporary Indonesian Painters.* Kuala Lumpur: Oxford University Press, 1994.

Wright, Astri. "The Emerging Herstory of Modern Art in Bali: The Seniwati Gallery for Women Artists." Presented at the Southeast Asia and the New Economic Order Conference, 6th Annual Conference of the Northwest Regional Consortium for Southeast Asian Studies, University of Washington, Seattle, 4–6 November 1994.

Works Cited

Wright, Astri. "Self-taught against the Grain: Three Contemporary Women Artists in Indonesia (and a Researcher from Abroad)." In May Datuin Flaudette and Patrick D. Flores, eds., *Women Imaging Women: Home, Body, Memory: Papers from the Conference on Artists from Indonesia, Philippines, Thailand, and Vietnam, Cultural Center of the Philippines, March 11–14, 1999*. Quezon City: Art Studies Foundation, 1999.

Index

Affandi, Kartika 62–63, 65
Agama Hindu Dharma (see Balinese Hinduism)
balian xxiii, 14, 35, 38, 45, 69
Balinese Hinduism 1, 20, 22, 24
Barong xxiii, 1, 4–5, 11, 13–14, 19, 22–25, 28, 41, 43–44, 58–60, 62
Blatjok, Ida Bagus Putu 41–42
Brahma 1, 59
Calonarang 2, 5, 13, 16, 18–19, 22, 25, 32, 39, 43, 57, 60, 64, 70
Covarrubias, Miguel xxi–xxii, 2, 16, 35, 58, 73
dance-drama xv, 19, 23–24, 37, 54, 62
Dewi Sri 26, 33, 38, 49
Durga 6, 9–10, 13–14, 16, 27, 33–35, 38, 40, 55, 58–59, 64
Erlangga 16–18
graveyard/cemetary 5–6, 13, 18, 27–28, 30–31, 35, 48, 51, 57
Gunawan, Hendra 5, 63, 75
Heraty, Toety 64
hell 20, 22, 56
holy water 24, 26, 43, 62
Kali 6, 13, 33–35, 40
karma 20, 22, 24–25, 31
Kawi 23
kris 23, 54, 62
lontar 17, 23, 65,
leyak xvi–xvii, 15–16, 25, 28, 31–33, 39–41, 43, 49–50, 57, 61, 72
Mahendradatta 7, 16–18, 24–26, 28, 38
Mpu Baradah 16–19, 22, 24, 27

Murnasih, I G.A.K. (Murni) xxii, 28, 32, 38, 48, 61, 67
pemangku xxiii, 18, 22, 28, 43, 45, 57, 72
pedanda xxiii, 27, 38, 53, 55, 69–70
poleng 11–12, 75
Pura Dalem 27–29, 40, 43, 51, 57, 73–74
Pura Desa 43
Pura Luhur 43–44
purgatory 20–21
Ramayana 56–57
Randeng Dirah 7, 16, 27, 54–55
Ratna Mengali 16–18, 65
Rawana 56–58
sakti 11, 28, 34,
Sanghyang Widi Wasa 1, 26, 33, 38, 60, 75
Sang Jogormanik 20–22
Sang Suratma 20–22
Shiva (see also Siwa) 34–35
Siwa 1, 5, 27, 55, 57–60
Spies, Walter xv–xvi, xxi, 2–3, 5–6, 9, 71
tenget 26
Tjeta, Ida Bagus Nyoman 7–8, 15, 48
Togog, Ida Bagus Made 23, 31
Trimurti 1
Vishnu (see Wisnu)
wayang kulit 5, 19
white cloth 2, 23, 49
widow 7, 9, 16–18, 27, 47–48, 50–54, 64
widow-witch xxii, 5, 7
Wisnu 1